Hello My Friend

Alee Peoples

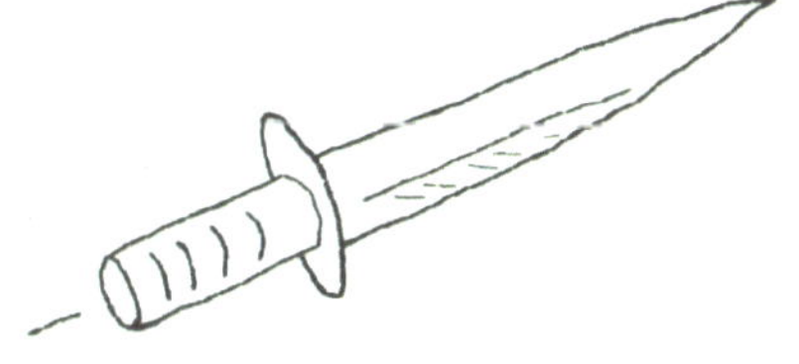

Hello My Friend

Insert Press
ISBN: 978-1-947322-06-6
Library of Congress Control Number: 2023937527

Published to accompany the exhibition Hello My Friend by Alee Peoples March 24 - June 3, 2023 at General Projects in the Lincoln Heights neighborhood of Los Angeles, CA.

A transcript of Episode 82 of The People with guests Alee Peoples and Cara Levine, hosted by Ben White and Mathew Timmons from January 18, 2020 is included at the back of this volume, beginning on page 49.

Type treatment on the front cover and title pages by Larry Snelly.
Design and Layout by Mathew Timmons.

Cover image: *I Find It Hard To Believe,* Alee Peoples, 2023.

Photography by David Weldzius.

Special thanks to Mike Stoltz.

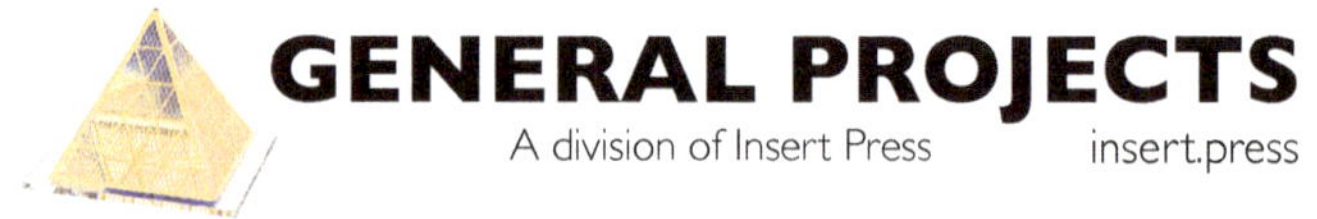

Hello My Friend

Alee Peoples

Essay by Ekrem Serdar

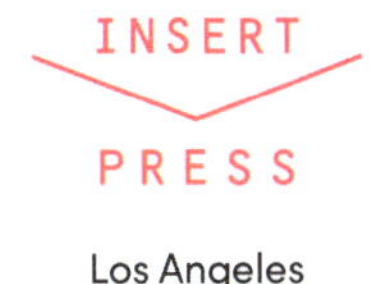

Los Angeles

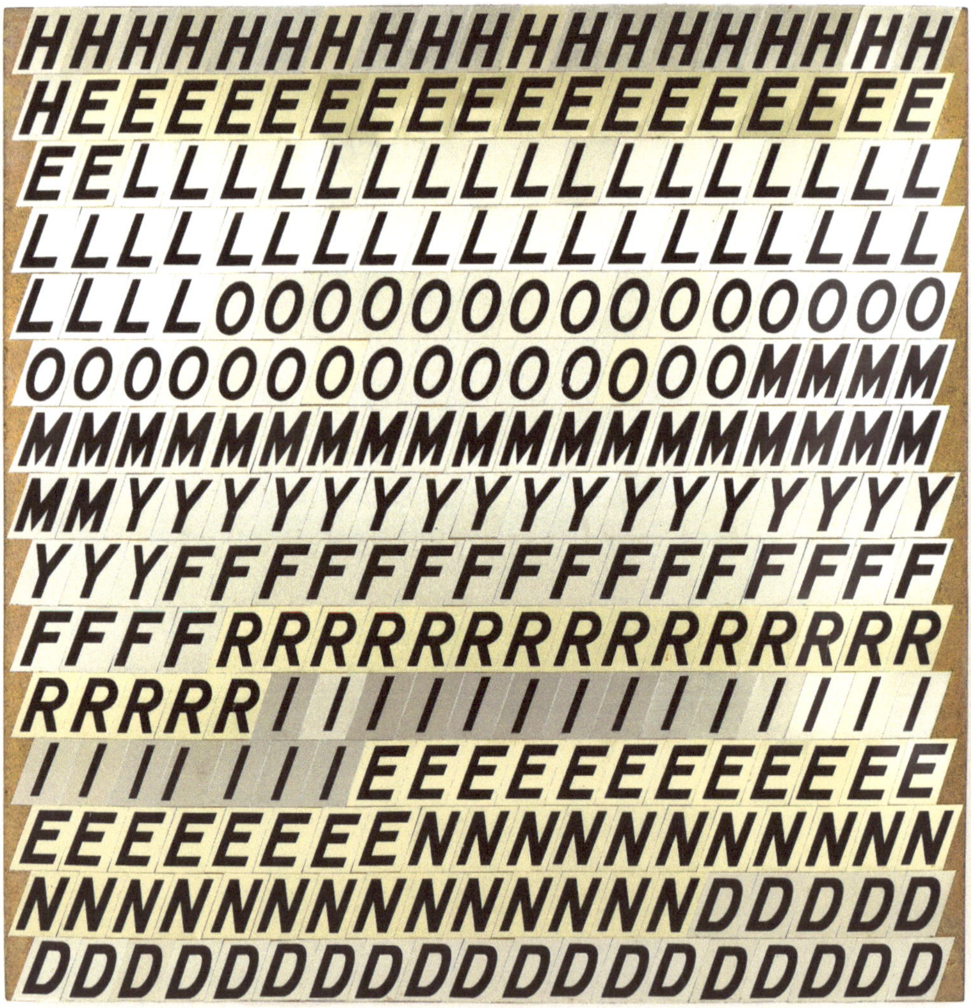

HHHHHHHHHHHHHHHHHHH
HEEEEEEEEEEEEEEEEEE
EELLLLLLLLLLLLLLLLL
LLLLLLLLLLLLLLLLLLL
LLLLOOOOOOOOOOOOOOO
OOOOOOOOOOOOOOOMMMM
MMMMMMMMMMMMMMMMMMM
MMYYYYYYYYYYYYYYYYY
YYYFFFFFFFFFFFFFFFF
FFFFRRRRRRRRRRRRRRR
RRRRRIIIIIIIIIIIIII
IIIIIIIEEEEEEEEEEEE
EEEEEEENNNNNNNNNNNN
NNNNNNNNNNNNNNDDDDD
DDDDDDDDDDDDDDDDDDD

Hello My Friend
Alee Peoples

General Projects
Lincoln Heights, Los Angeles, CA

March 24 - June 3, 2023

Alee Peoples is an innovative multimedia artist whose work explores the intersections of text, pattern, and visual communication. Her work is like a Rubik's Cube, deceptively simple and fascinating. Shooting Super 8 and 16mm in her film work and using repurposed fabric and materials in her textile work, Peoples transforms everyday objects into unique, abstract narratives that explore the absurdities and banalities of our contemporary imagination. Elements of a cosmic aesthetic run throughout her work, bringing her handcrafted look to life. Her work engages in a fierce form of play, grappling with meaning instead of grasping for it.

Alee Peoples maintains a varied artistic practice that involves screen-printing, sewing, sculpture and film. Currently living in Los Angeles, she has taught youth classes at Echo Park Film Center and shown her sculpture and film work at GAIT, 4th Wall and Elephant Art Space. Peoples has shown her films at numerous festivals including Edinburgh, Images (Toronto) and New York Film Festival, and at museums and spaces including SFMoMA, Brooklyn Museum of Art, The Pompidou Center, Dirt Palace (Providence) and The Nightingale (Chicago). Started in 2022, Arroyo Seco Cine Club is a thematically programmed film series she co-curates with Mike Stoltz. She is inspired by pedestrian histories, pop song lyrics and is invested in the handmade.

Perceiving the Parts, Observing the Whole

Ekrem Serdar

Gathering an emblematic selection of sculpture, film, painting, textile, metal, and graphic work from nearly twenty years of practice, *Hello My Friend* features Alee Peoples' work of criss-crossed signals and evocative play. Peoples works with legible materials and codes, to "unpack… explode… [or] veil"[1] how we encounter them, in and through our day to day lives. In the influential classic *Understanding Comics* (1993)[2] Scott McCloud defines the phenomenon of closure as "observing the parts and perceiving the whole." Drawing from common consumer goods, drive-by capitalist ephemera, and a turn of phrase to turn them over and inside out, Peoples' work holds our minds at a point where closure is always emerging and ever receding.

Peoples' stated "dedication to the handmade" is a significant aspect threading together the different mediums she works in. While we may naturally associate the term with textiles, it is similarly important to consider the many filmmakers, film workers, and media histories that have taken up the mantle or could be thought of in the oft-ignored and gendered labor of *craft*. The connections between textile and film go back to some of the foundations of the moving image: The Lumiere brothers, trying to find a way to have individual frames move consistently across the lens, integrated the intermittent mechanism of the sewing machine after seeing it in a dream, and this mechanism is what forms the illusion of movement in our eyes.[3] The connection

1 Insert Press, "Episode 82: Alee Peoples and Cara Levine", The People Radio, https://soundcloud.com/insertpress/ep-82-alee-peoples-and-cara-levine-the-people, January 18, 2020. [See page 49 for transcript]

2 This was shared by the artist as we discussed her exhibition.

3 Louis Lumiere, "The Lumière Cinematograph", ed. Raymond Fielding, *A Technological History of Motion Pictures and Television: An Anthology from the Pages of the Journal of the Society of Motion Picture and Television Engineers*, University of California Press, 1984.

between these two industrial forms continued over the course of their long histories: Film producers often hired women to take on the work of editing, dyeing film, seeing the work similar to the gendered labor of sewing, knitting, and other textile work.[4] This connection was brought into focus in Dziga Vertov's film *Man with a Movie Camera* (1929), edited by Yelizaveta Svilova who was married to the director. Svilova intercuts the work of women workers in a textile factory, with footage of her editing the film we are watching; in regards to the film, the artist Hito Steyerl acutely asked why the film wasn't named *The Woman At the Editing Desk.*[5] Not dissimilar to Svilova's labor, Peoples edits her film work on rewinds with a splicer, the individual 16mm film frames less than half an inch wide, seconds passing across her eyes as her hands roll the film back and forth, looking closely, cutting, splicing. What may seem a linear format, in Peoples' hands, becomes as three dimensional, as textural as her textile work. The connection is perhaps most evident in Peoples' work *BIG TIME* (2020), a framed work made of individual film frames that spell the title. The play in the work registers on several levels: the film frames are from 70 mm and 35 mm film (with BIG spelled entirely in 70 mm), theatrical film gauges as opposed to the 16mm film gauge Peoples' uses in her own work. Thinking through time, one is both confronted with the individual frames and their non-linearity—which, if they were laid progressively and projected at 24 frames per second, would amount to ~10 seconds.

The latest of her film work included in the exhibition, *Standing Forward Full* (2020), is reminiscent of Hollis Frampton's 1970 linguistic city symphony *Zorn's Lemma* in how both share a wonderful dry humor and wordplay.

---

4 More information about women film editors can be found in sources including the website *Edited By*, by Su Friedrich. https://womenfilmeditors.princeton.edu/

5 Joey Huertas, *Esther Shub films introduced by writer Hito Steyerl*, https://vimeo.com/51055818, documentation from the event Esfir Shub's *The Fall of the Romanov Dynasty* at Light Industry (NYC), October 8, 2012.

The film begins with a series of letters, numbers, and words variously written and found on a cardboard box on a street, written in cursive on an ipad, found in a note in a pocket, a button on a DVD player. The words spell out “Instead of scrying: your self 2 sleep assume standing FWD full”. This is followed by a performer who obeys this direction, and bends onto all fours, upon which the film goes through a series of images and scenes opposing “scrying,” from people kissing, the filmmaker going down a slide, to a band performing at the end, and what the filmmaker calls “an exorcism attempt of an unrequited desire.” The gorgeous, *Domino Face* (2022), one of Peoples’ most recent banner works, shows a flowing side of a domino, and its title, reminiscent of an insult, ties in the acute and direct way that Peoples’ plays with both language and image, while *I Find It Hard to Believe* (2023) brings magic and tricks into the fold as a way to think through Peoples’ works: a knife, in unlikely flight, but its veracity confirmed by its reflection on the water. A similar joy is found in the mechanical movement of the mannequins repeated by the performers in *Non-Stop Beautiful Ladies* (2015) which is reminiscent of Stuart Sherman’s work in its sheer inventiveness. Writing this essay, I return again and again to images of *Hello My Friend* (2016), titling the exhibition, reading the individual sign letters, out loud in every way I can, a long breathy “h” at the beginning, sometimes just starting with the “i” in “friend.” *Vast Time / See You Later* (2023) invites a similar but encompassingly tongue in cheek linguistic participation with the word VAST, jaggedly going up the banner, bones laid out along the sides, and an hourglass with seemingly little sand left to let us know we may have to see each other later. Along two of the main walls in the gallery, *Identity Strip* (2003–ongoing), is composed of numerous expired credit cards, library cards, phone cards, and saver cards turned towards the wall so only the back sides are visible. Each of these cards—unique to a certain place, business or civic entity, and particular to a specific time in one’s life—are on exhibit here with one long data swipe of a black strip poking at the absurd and all-encompassing nature of consumer culture.

In an interview with Clint Enns,[6] Peoples remarks on comedy that "[i]t allows us to feel human again. One of humor's greatest strengths can be considered a political strategy: it brings people together through the sharing of a laugh... Conventional comedy is difficult for me since it follows formulas that are rarely deviated from. It is when these formulas are ignored that humor begins to work. I've always disliked jokes because it's expected that you laugh after the second or third line, a form of call and response." This togetherness is what the artist, and her exhibition, *Hello My Friend*, ultimately invites: To talk, joke, chat, imagine, and play with you, as opposed to at you, the passive consumer. Her transformative, evocative work invites the same participation you may have among friends, opposing the expected and ultimately harmful closures of capitalist culture, and rejoicing together in the infinite gift of shared camaraderie. *See you soon.*

6 Clint Enns, "How to Keep Your Eyes Wide Open All the Time: An Interview with Alee Peoples", *INCITE Journal*, https://www.incite-online.net/peoples.html , 2017.

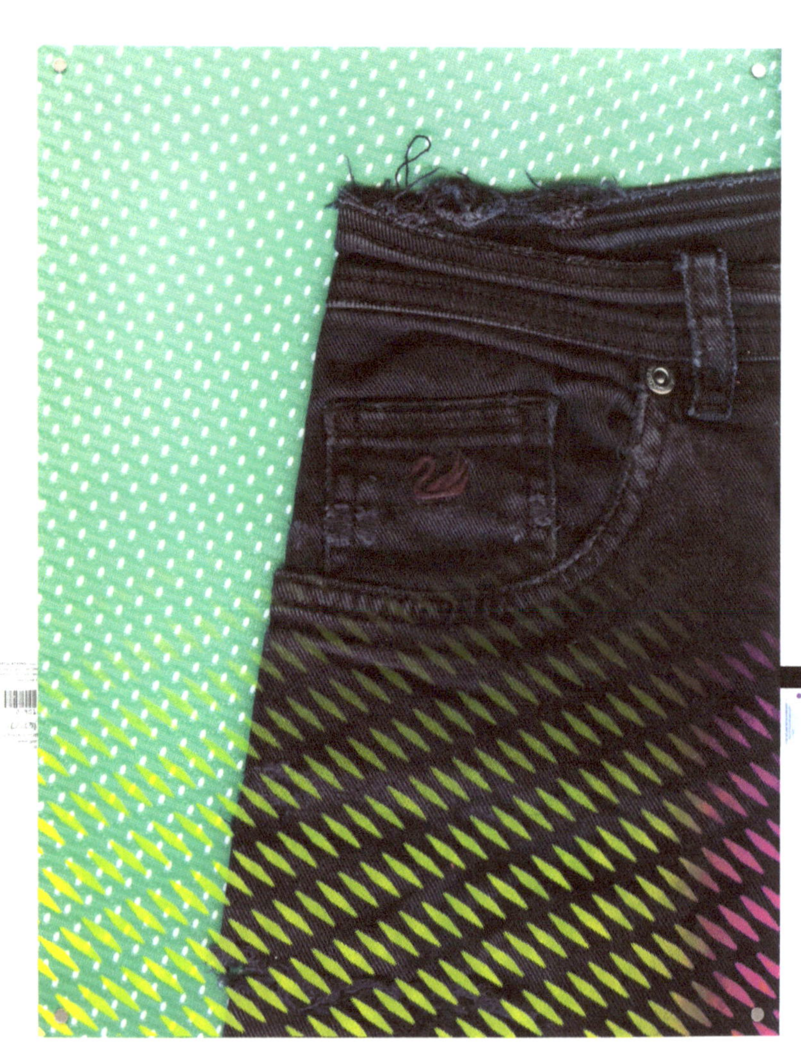
PUBLIC SAFETY (401) 277 4848

Installation

Hello My Friend

Alee Peoples

counter-clockwise from entrance

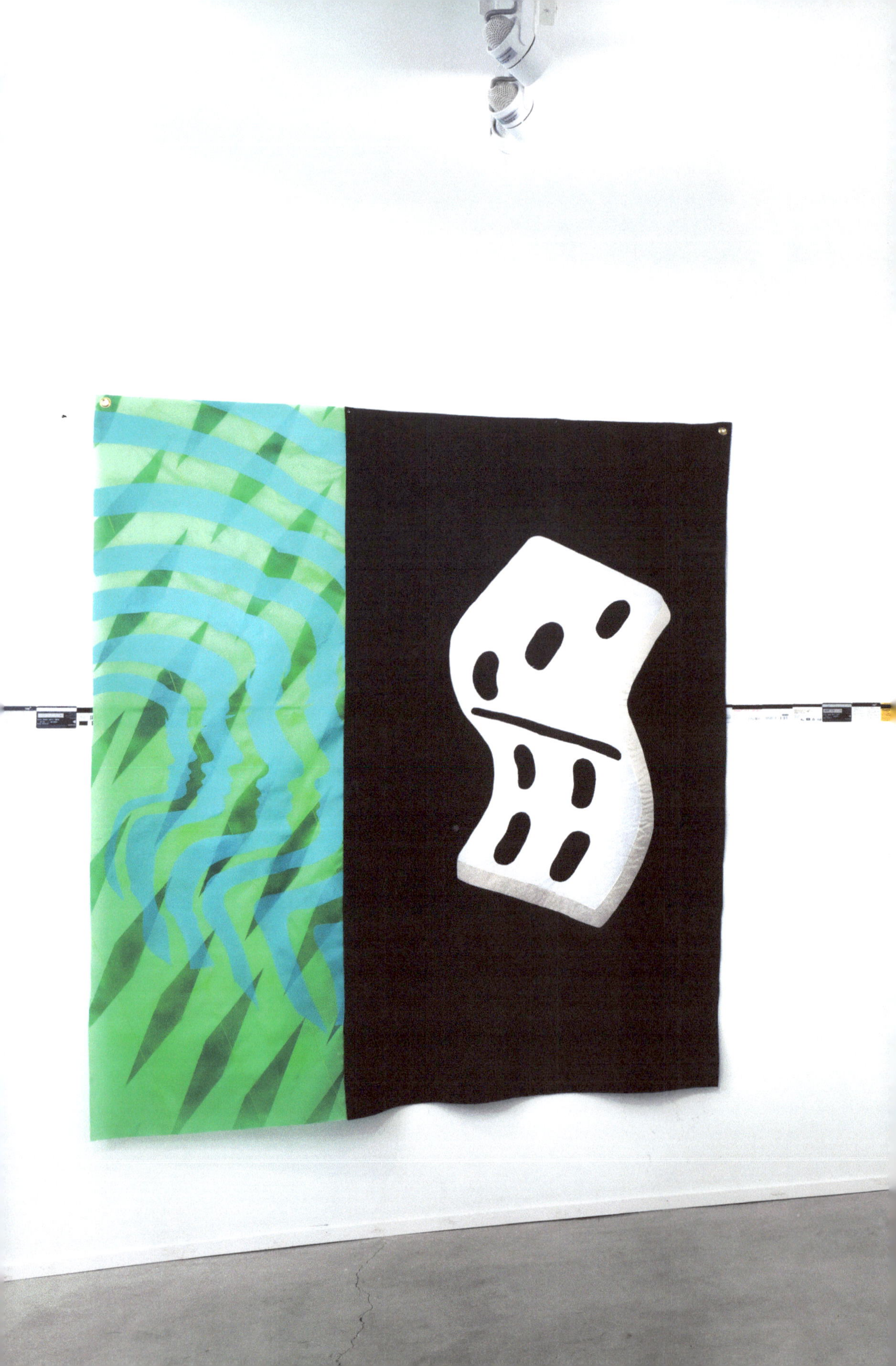

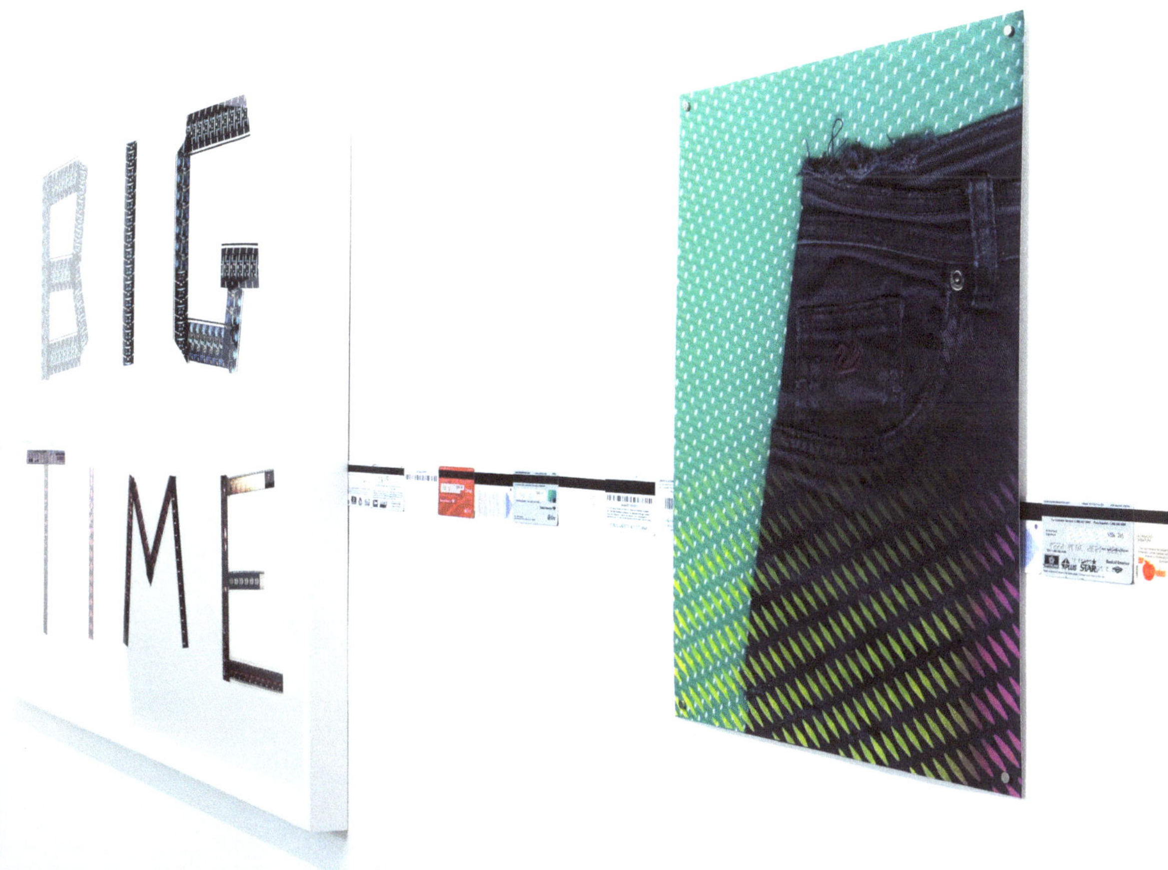
BIG
TIME

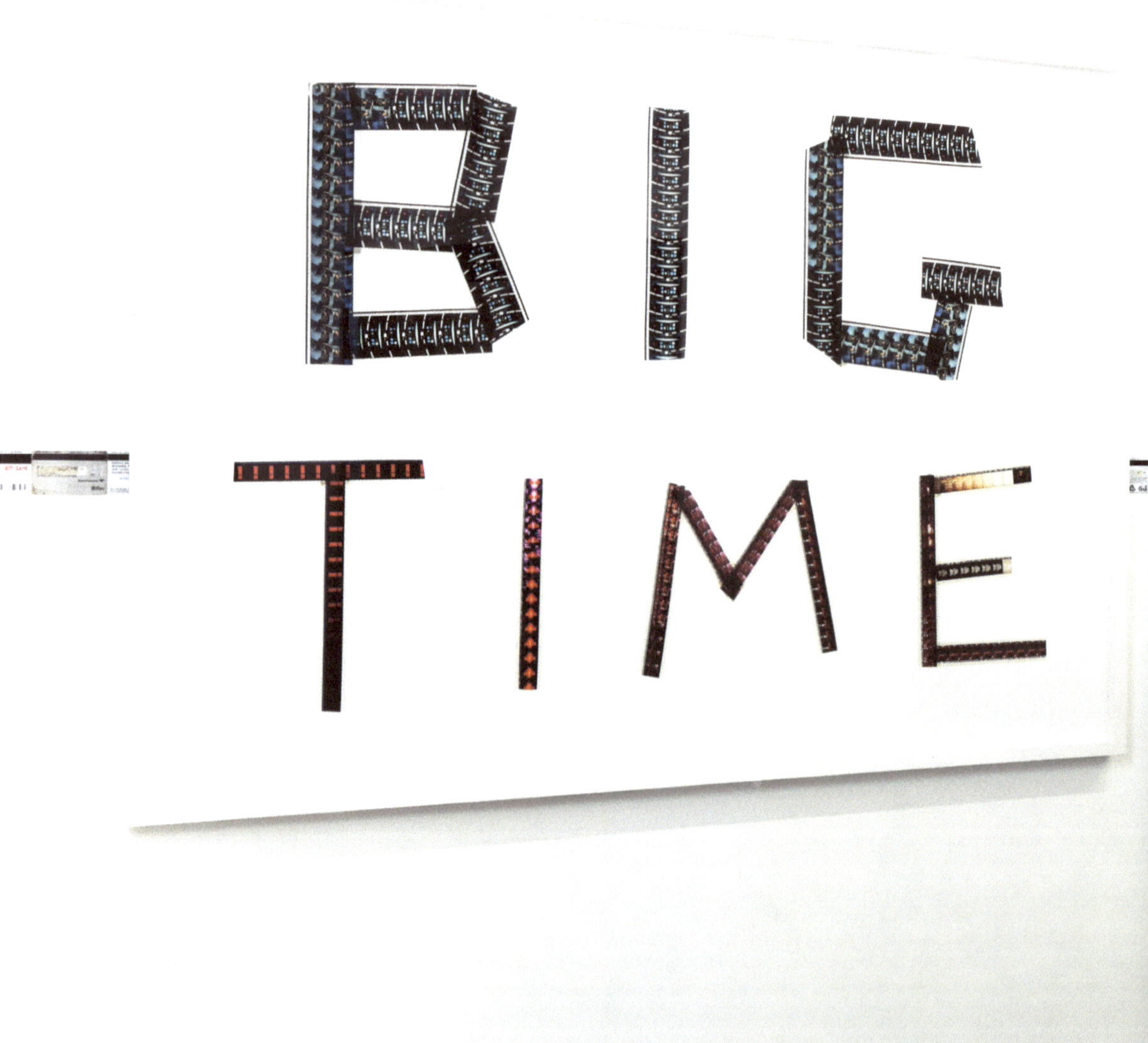
BIG
TIME

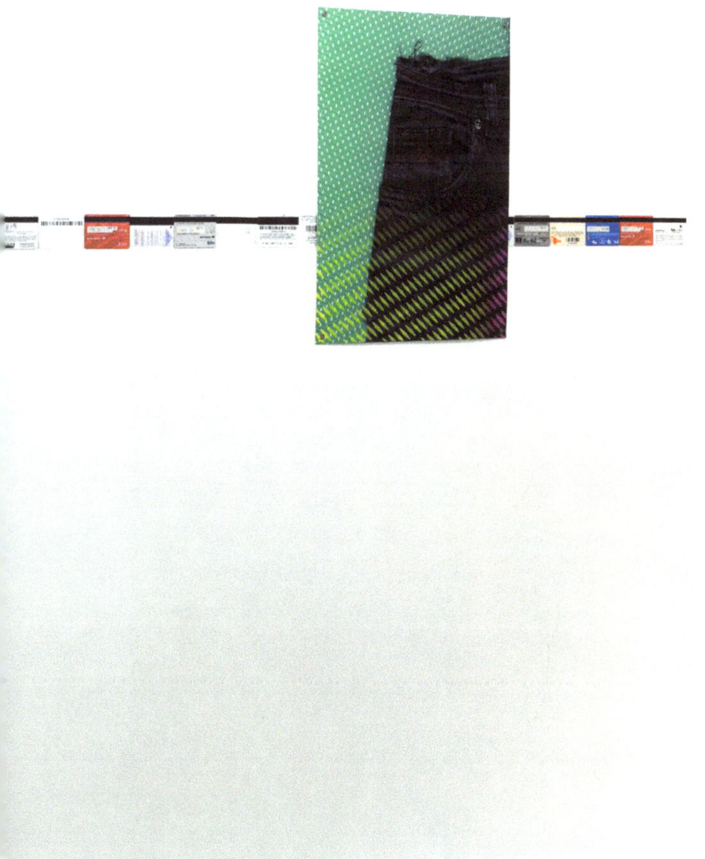

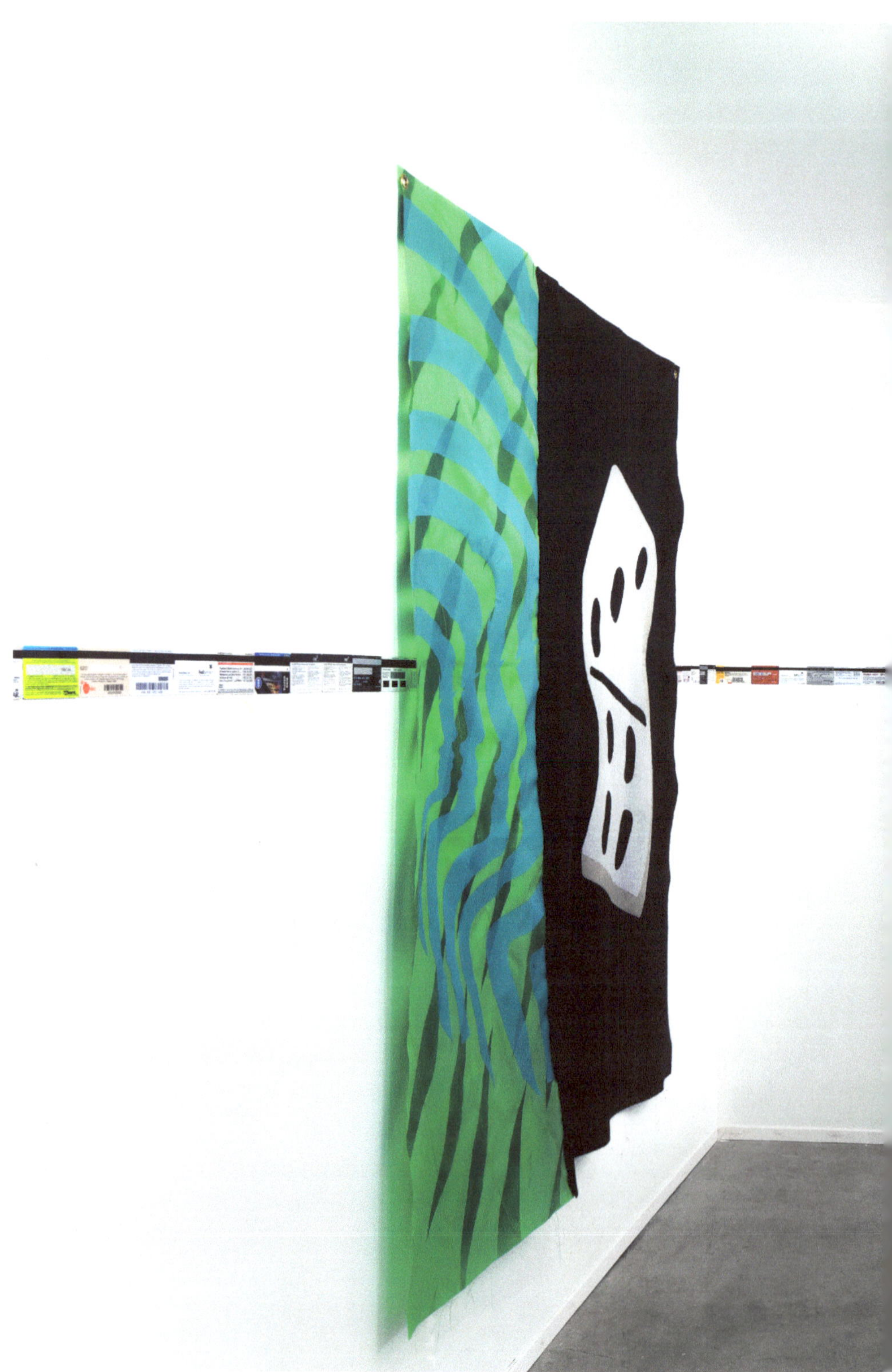

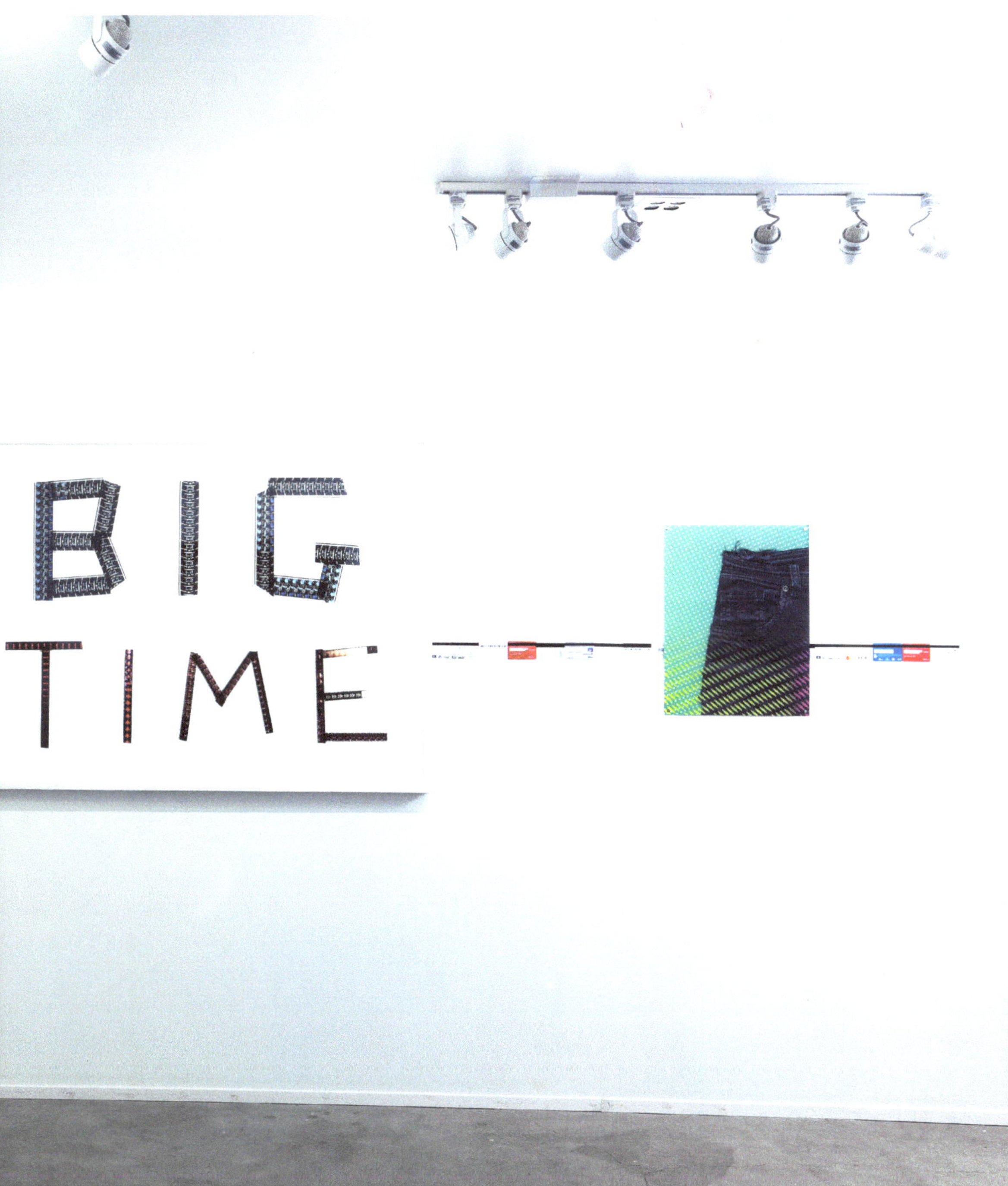
BIG
TIME

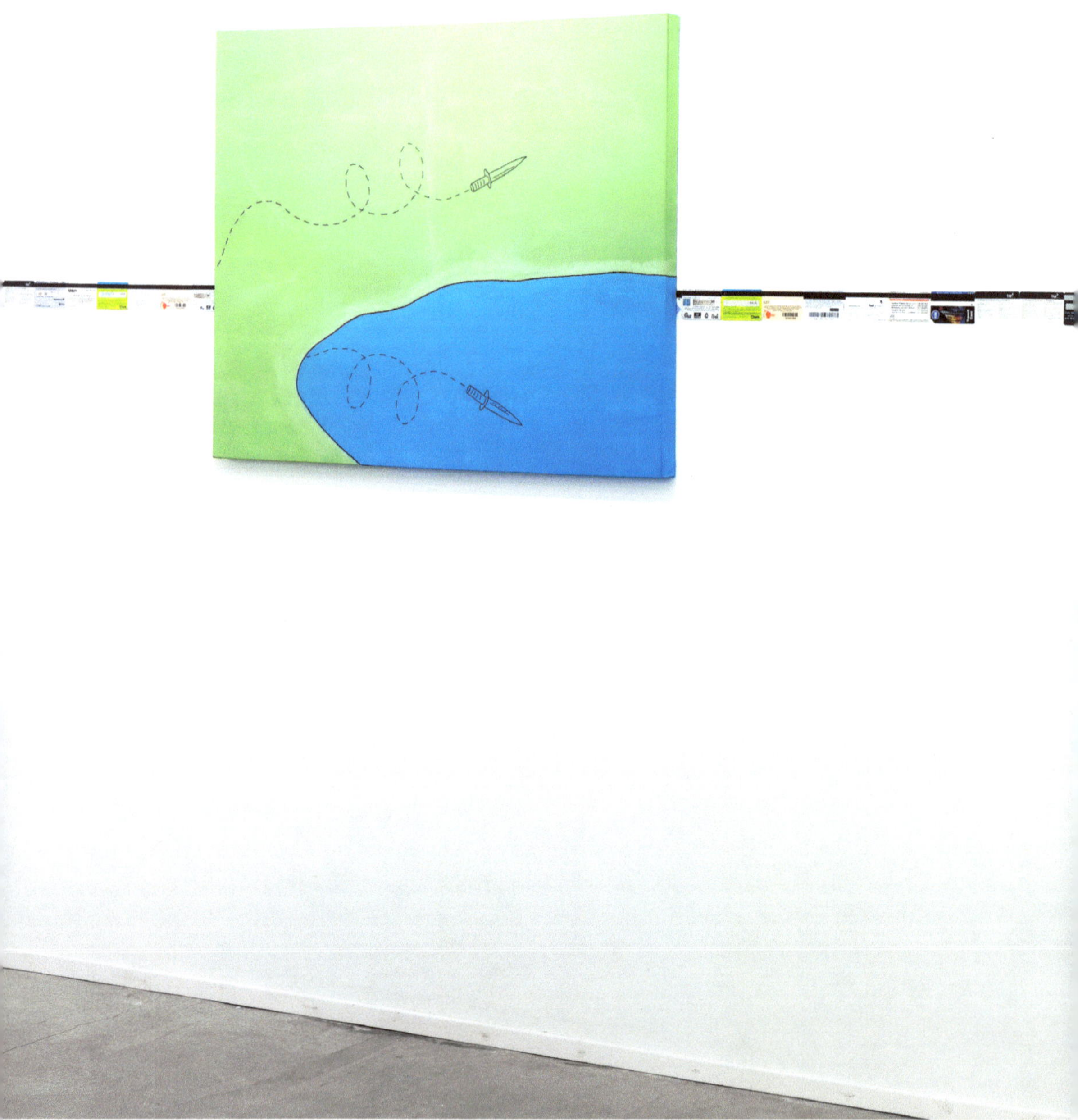

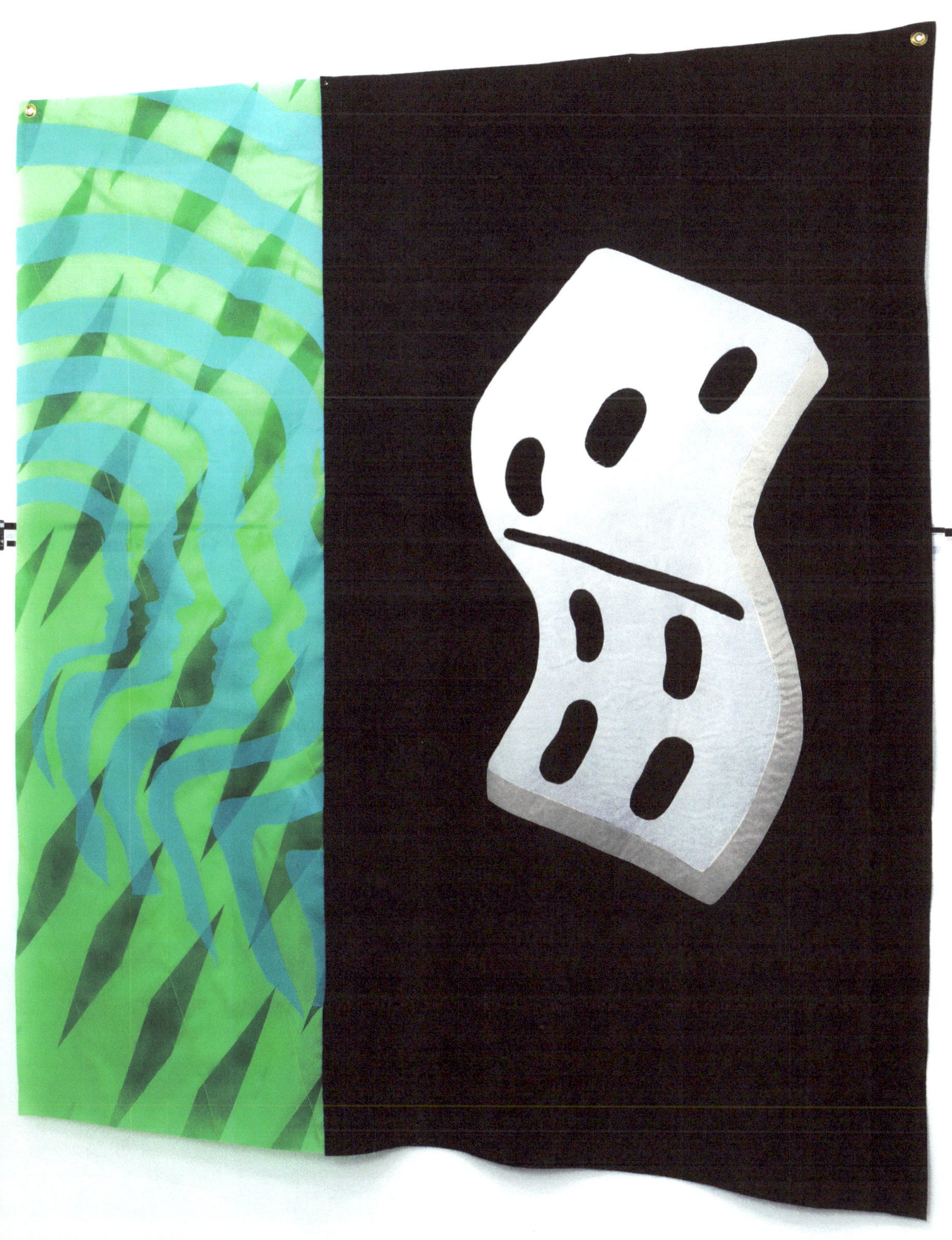

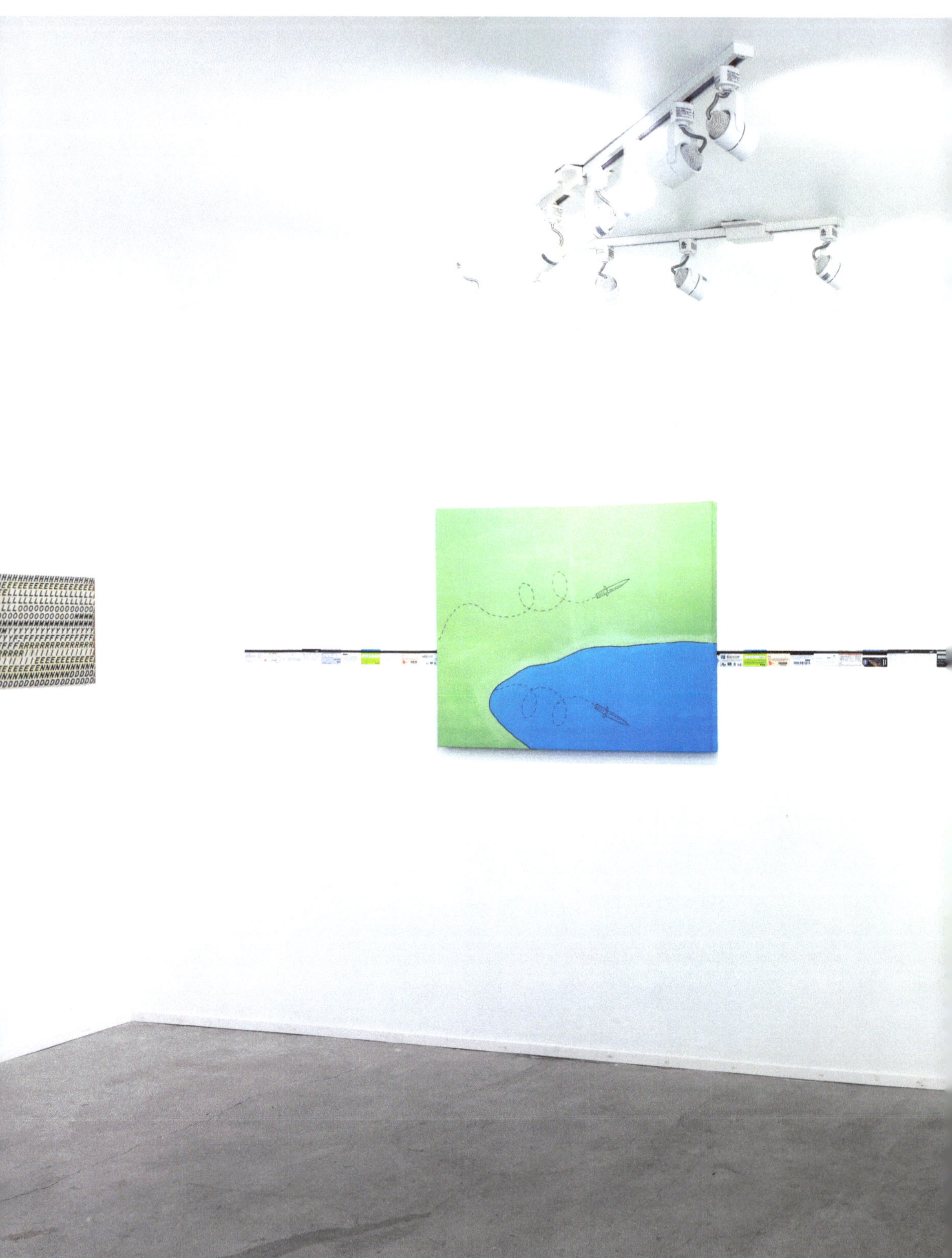

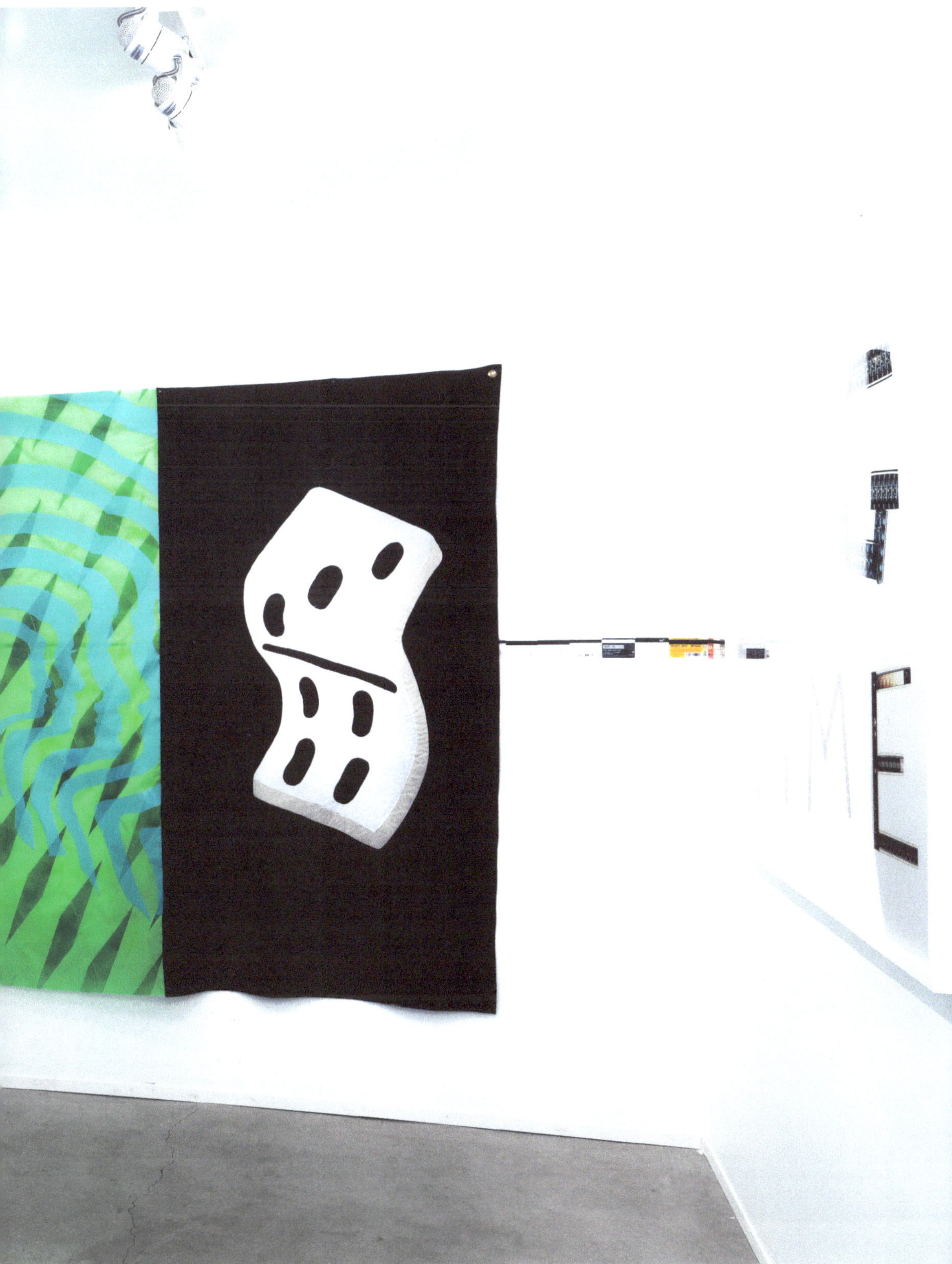

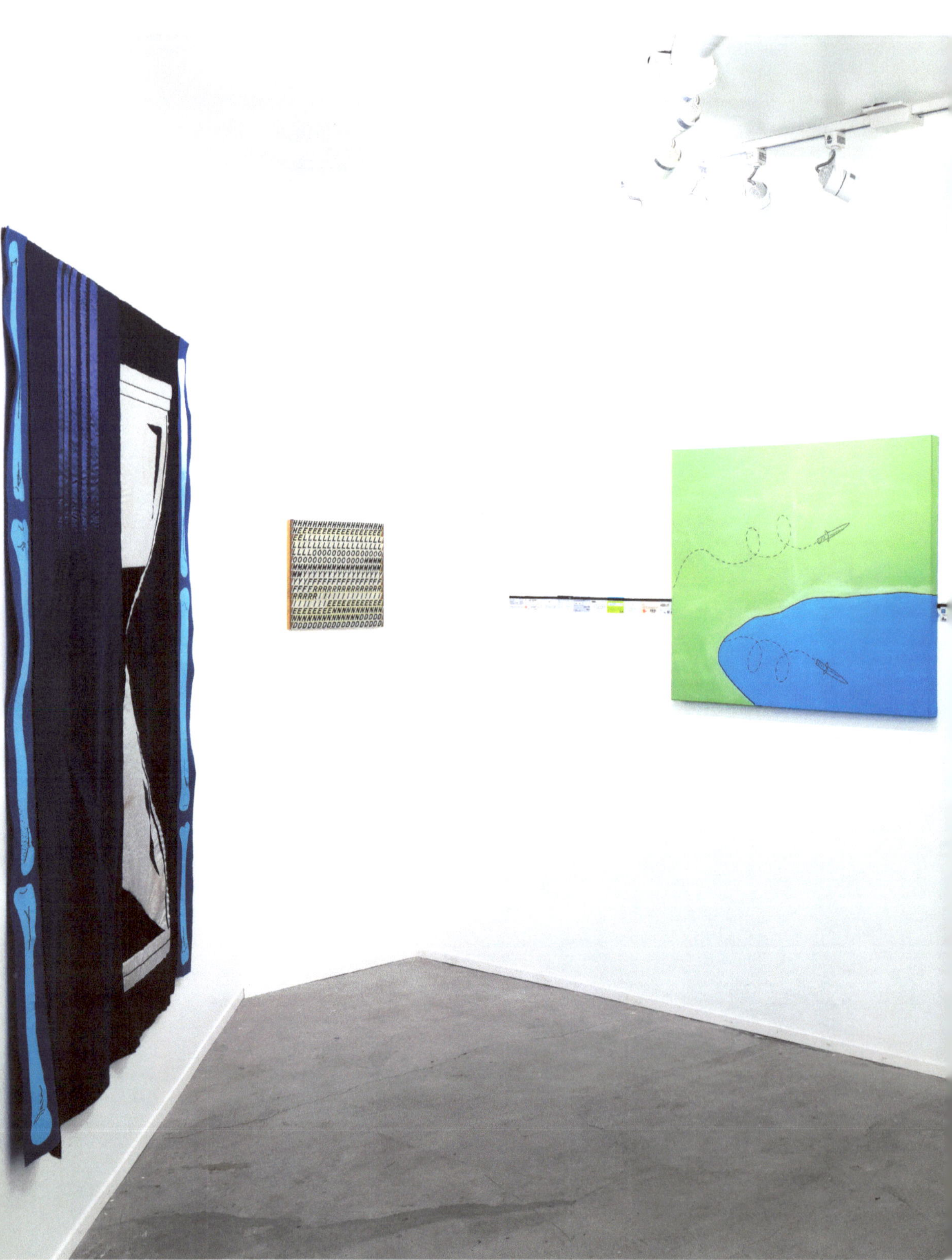

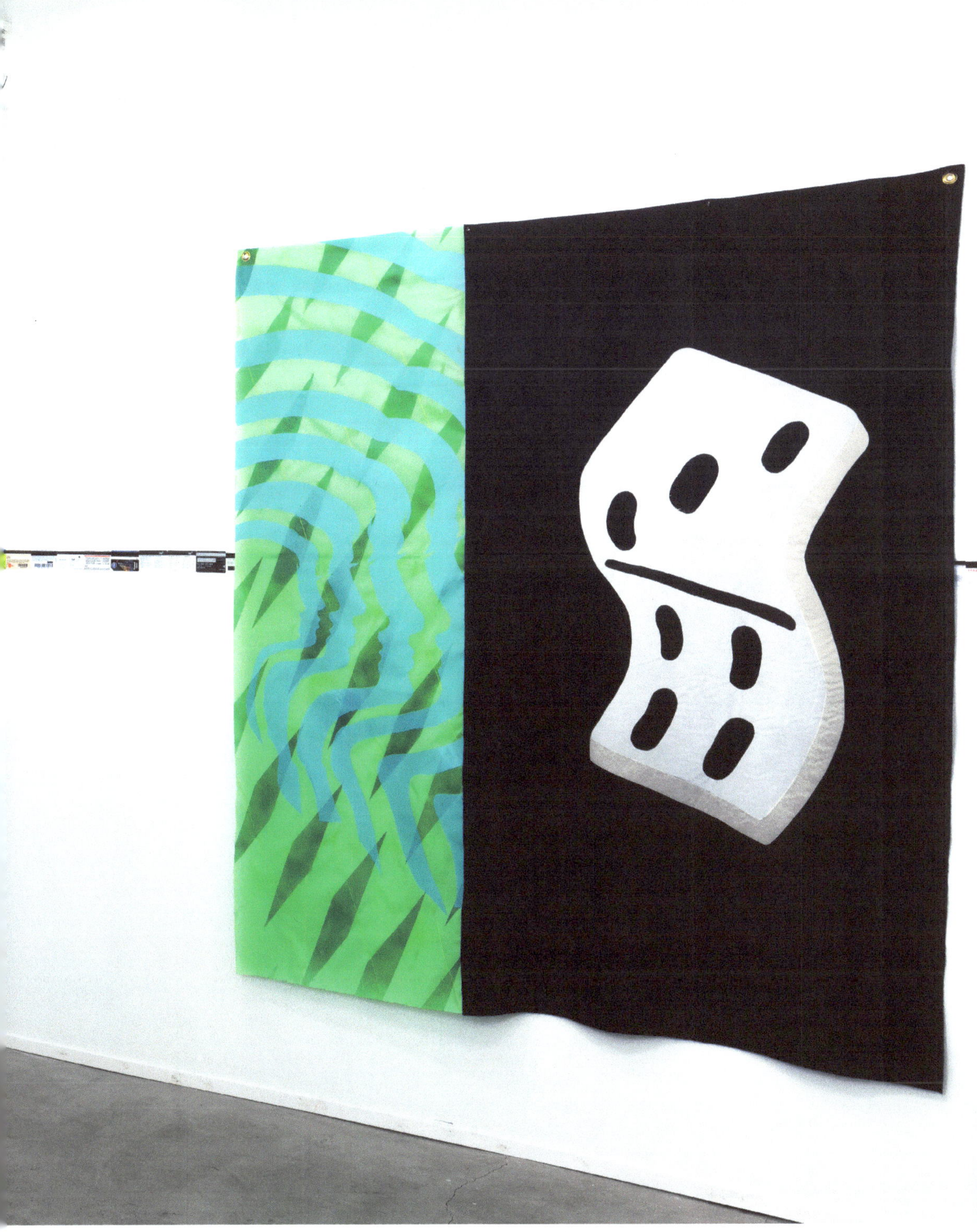

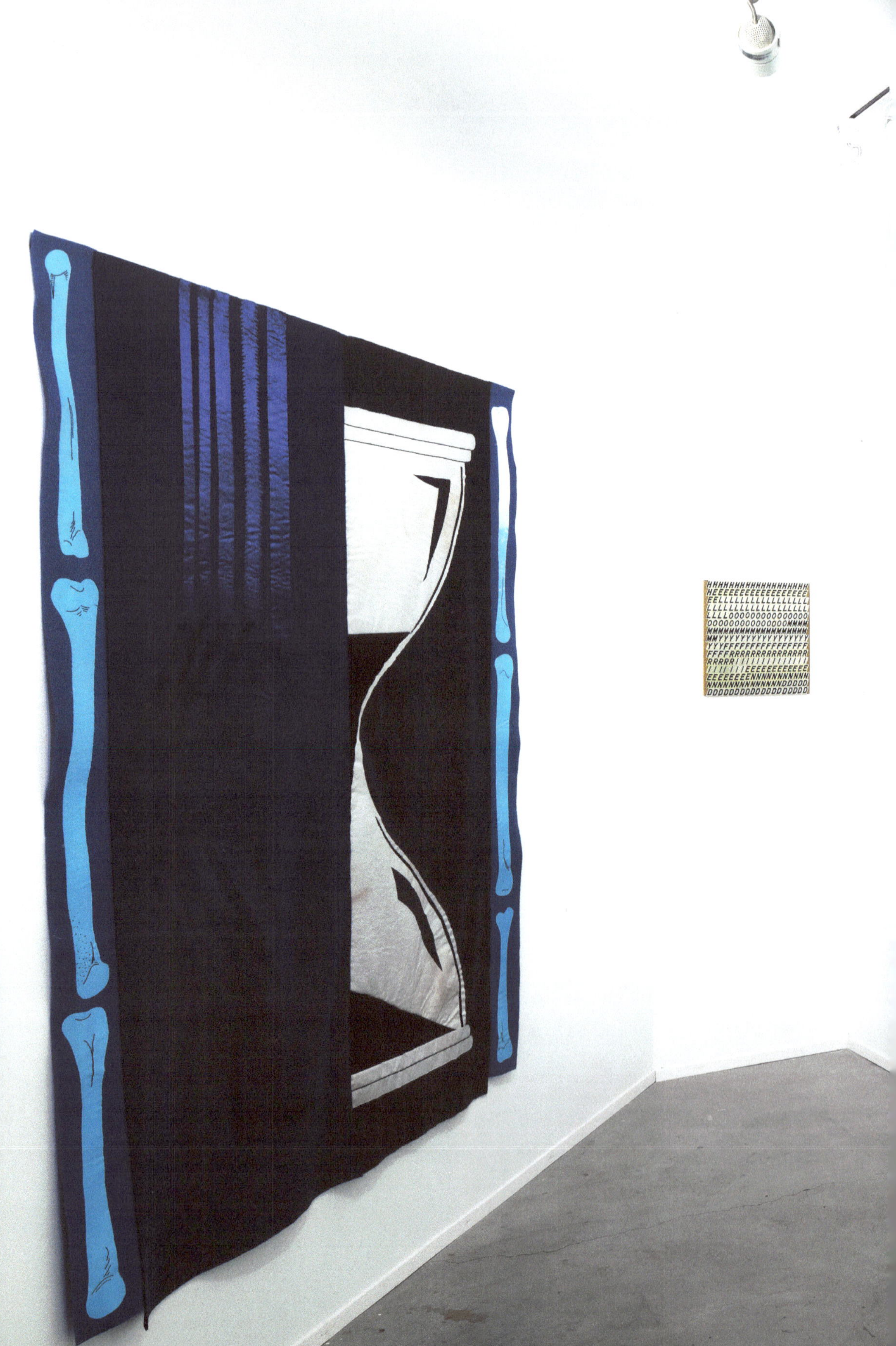
HHHHHHHHHHHHHHHHHHH
HEEEEEEEEEEEEEEEEEE
EELLLLLLLLLLLLLLLLL
LLLLLLLLLLLLLLLLLLL
LLLLOOOOOOOOOOOOOOO
OOOOOOOOOOOOOOOMMMM
MMMMMMMMMMMMMMMMMMM
MMYYYYYYYYYYYYYYYYY
YYYFFFFFFFFFFFFFFFF
FFFFRRRRRRRRRRRRRRR
RRRRRIIIIIIIIIIIIII
IIIIIIIEEEEEEEEEEEE
EEEEEEEENNNNNNNNNNN
NNNNNNNNNNNNNNDDDDD
DDDDDDDDDDDDDDDDDDD

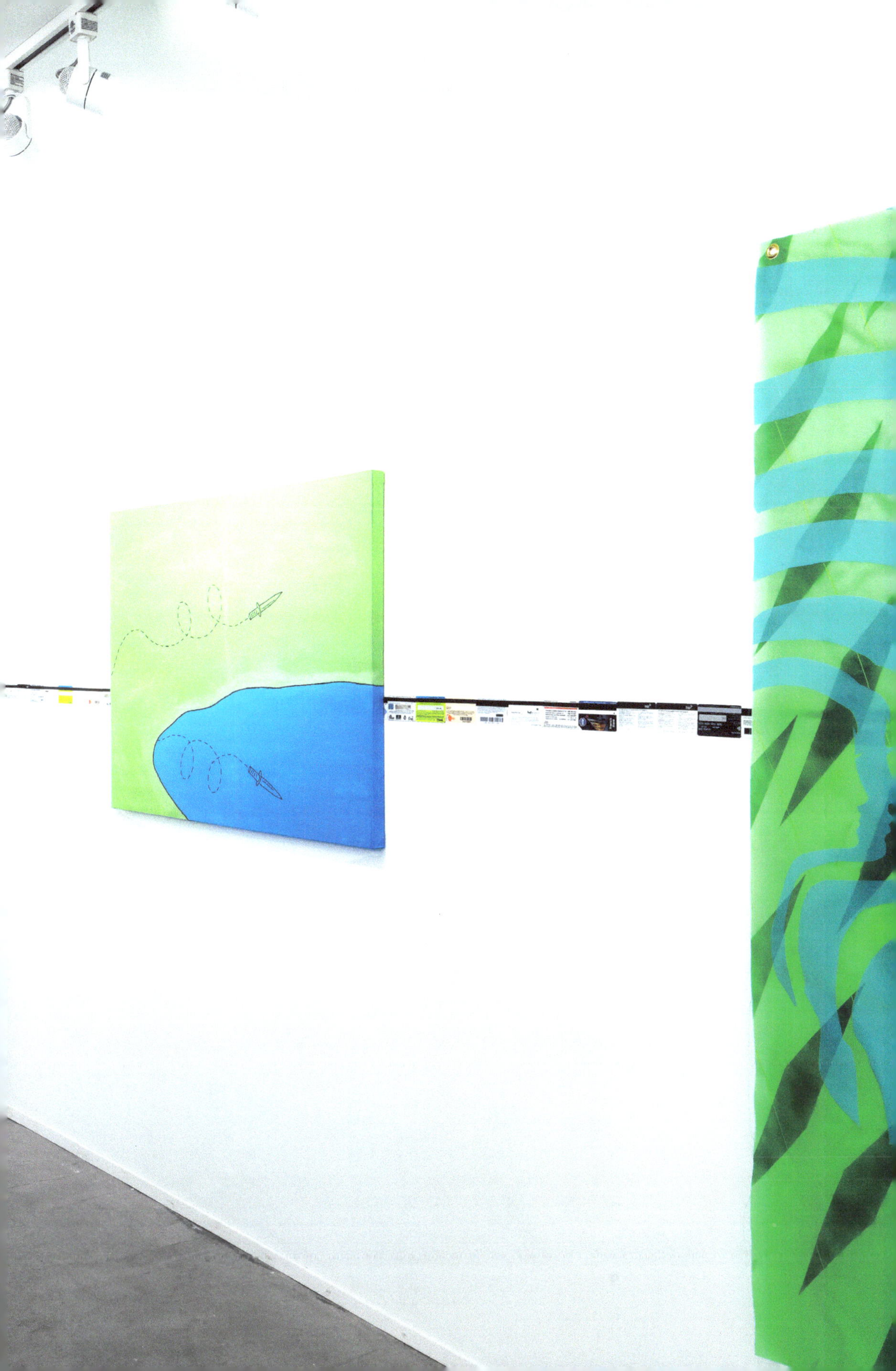

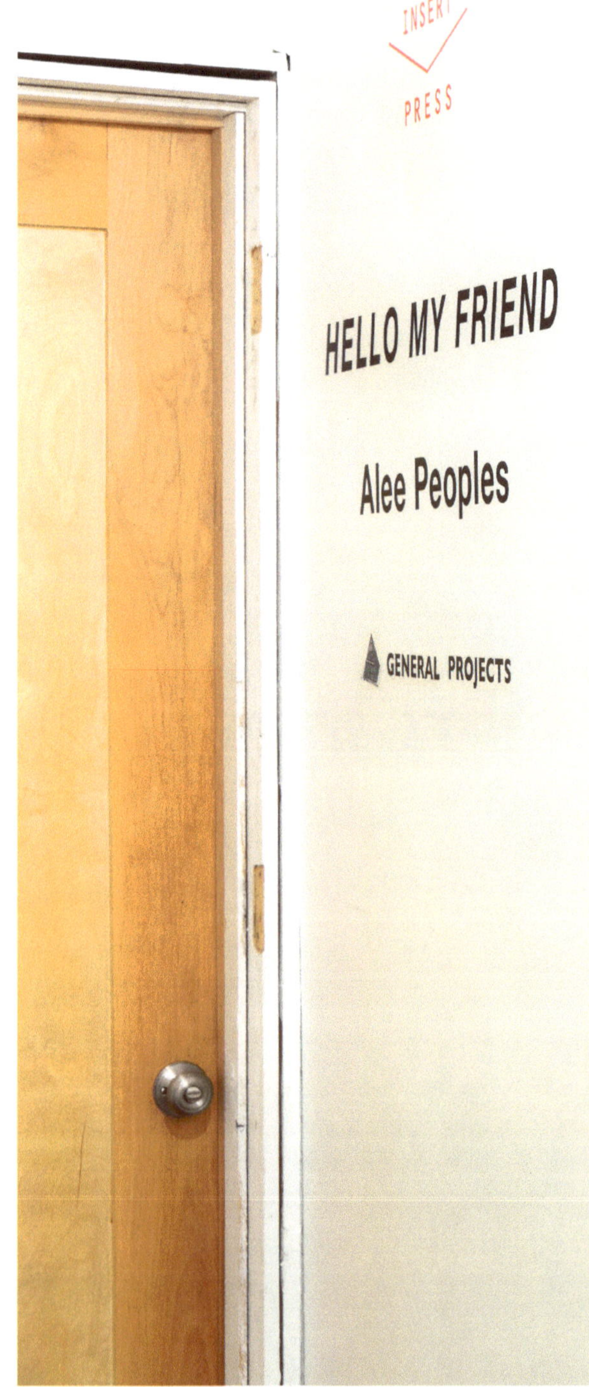
INSERT
PRESS
HELLO MY FRIEND
Alee Peoples
GENERAL PROJECTS

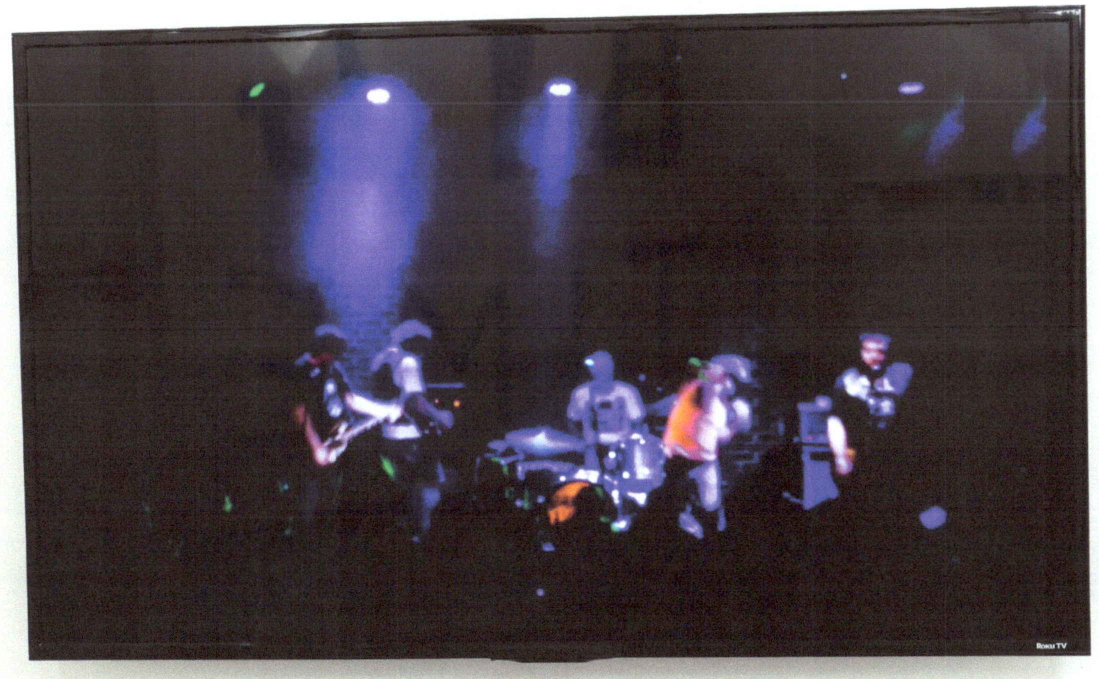
Roku TV

Individual Works

Hello My Friend

Alee Peoples

counter-clockwise from entrance

Identity Strip
Alee Peoples, 2003-ongoing
Plastic cards and adhesive
2-1/8" x variable dimensions

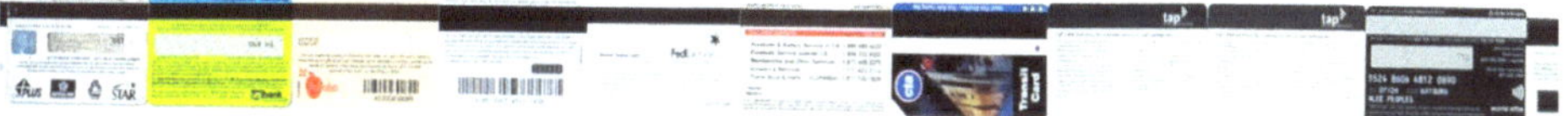

Caroline's Jeans
Alee Peoples, 2023
Silkscreen Monoprint
onto an Archival InkJet print
on 21mil Epson Cold Press Bright paper
22" x 17"
Edition of 25 plus 4 A.P.'s

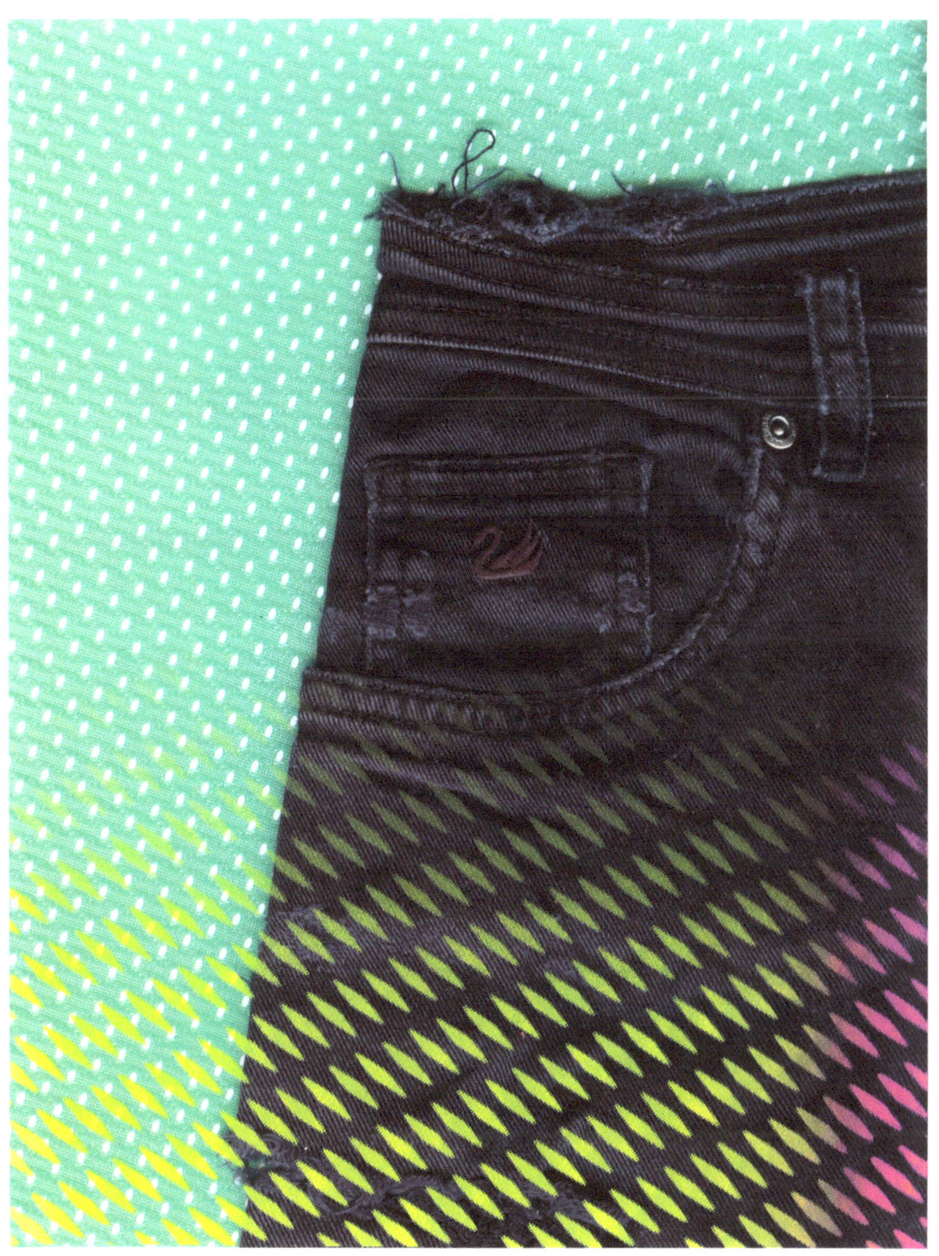

BIG TIME
Alee Peoples, 2020
Archival InkJet print
41-1/2" x 56"

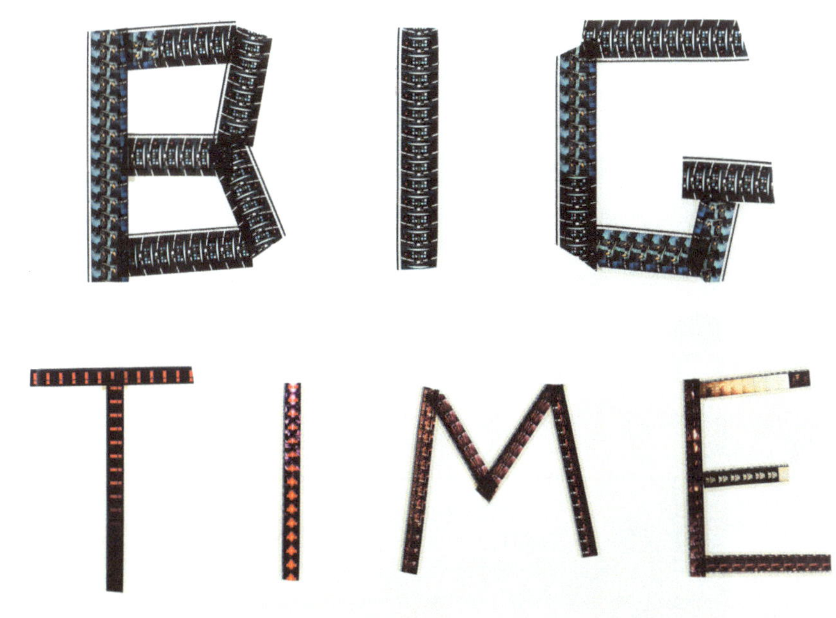
BIG
TIME

Domino Face

Alee Peoples, 2022

Wool, satin, nylon, acrylic, thread

70" x 62"

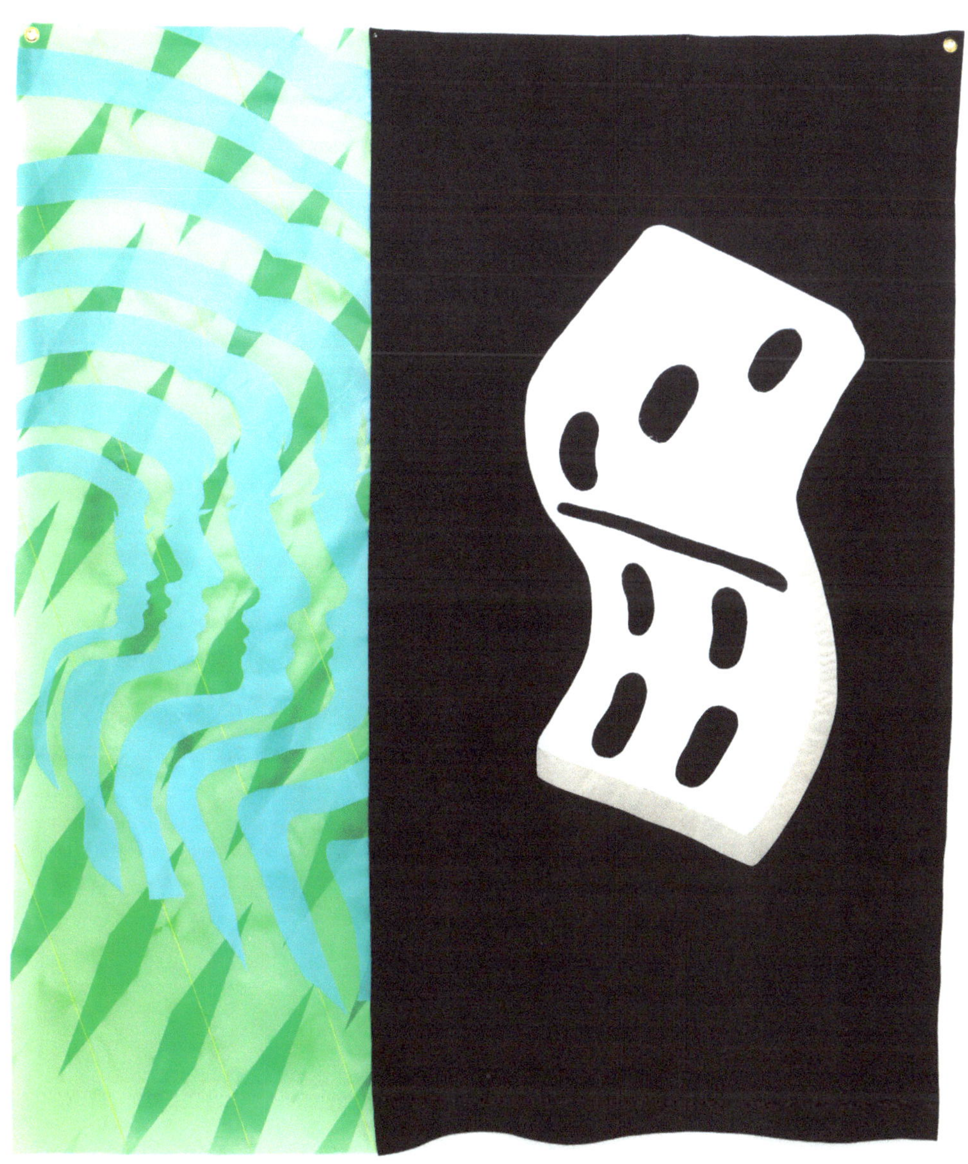

I Find It Hard To Believe

Alee Peoples, 2023

Acrylic and hand embroidery on canvas

32″ x 42″

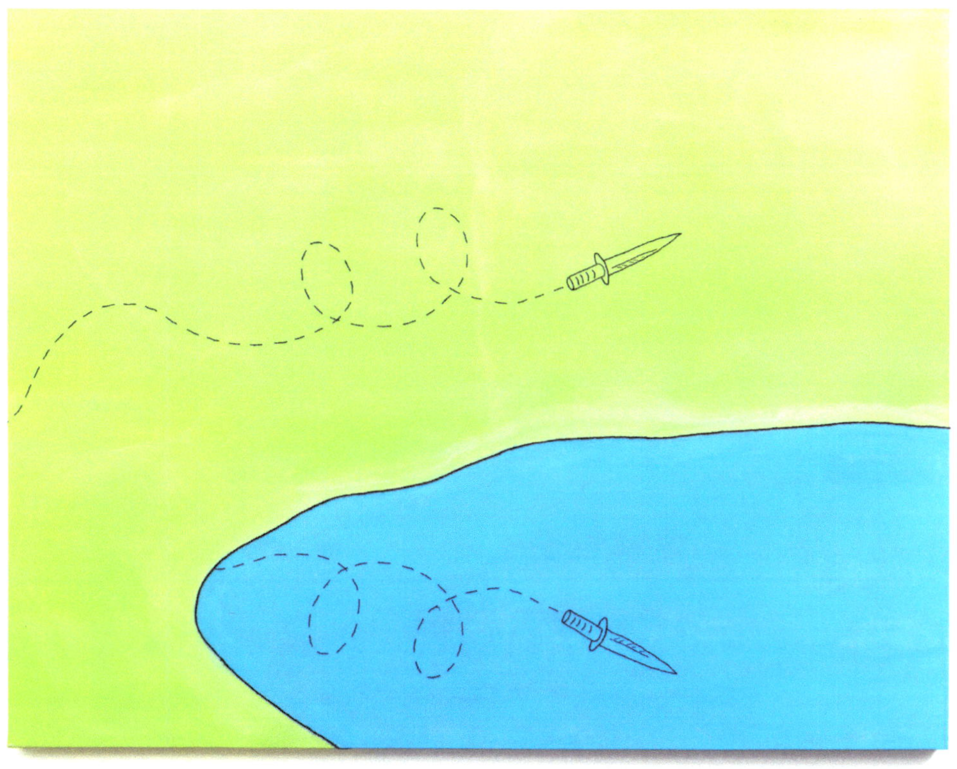

Hello My Friend

Alee Peoples, 2016

Metal sign letters and acrylic on masonite

16" x 14"

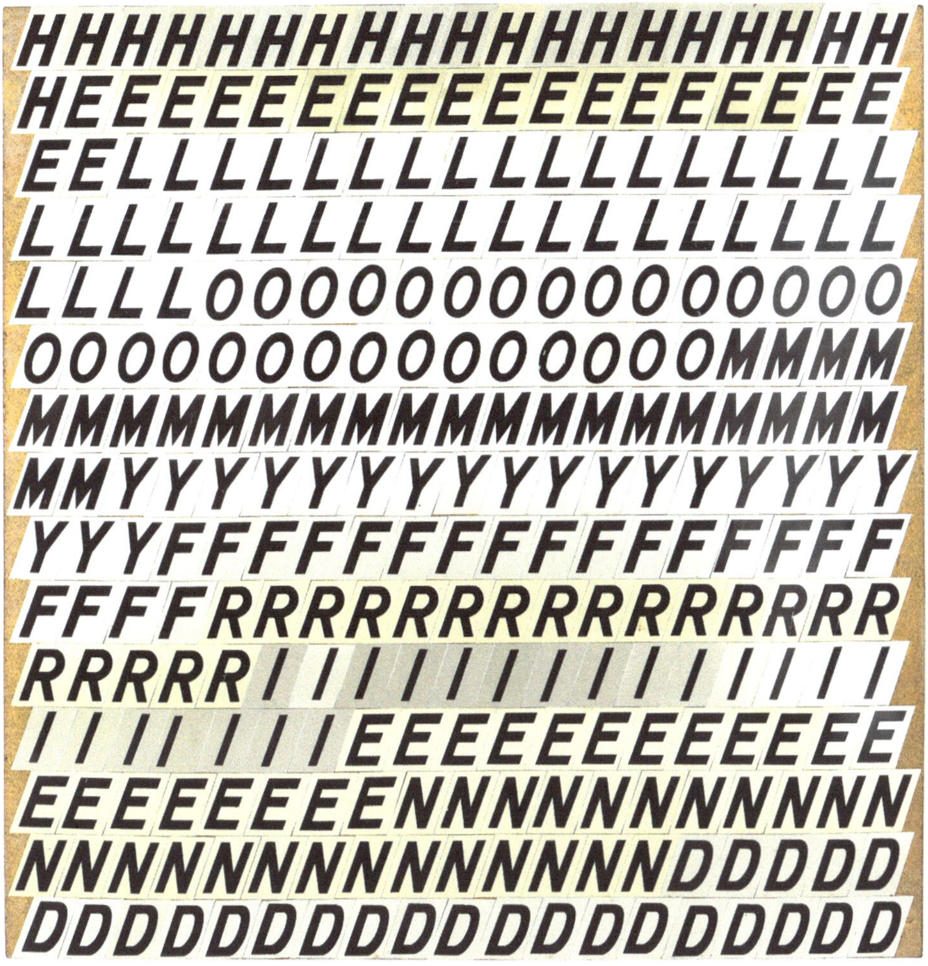
HHHHHHHHHHHHHHHHHHH
HEEEEEEEEEEEEEEEEEE
EELLLLLLLLLLLLLLLLL
LLLLLLLLLLLLLLLLLLL
LLLLOOOOOOOOOOOOOOO
OOOOOOOOOOOOOOOMMMM
MMMMMMMMMMMMMMMMMMM
MMYYYYYYYYYYYYYYYYY
YYYFFFFFFFFFFFFFFFF
FFFFRRRRRRRRRRRRRRR
RRRRRIIIIIIIIIIIIII
IIIIIIIEEEEEEEEEEEE
EEEEEEENNNNNNNNNNNN
NNNNNNNNNNNNNNDDDDD
DDDDDDDDDDDDDDDDDDD

Vast Time / See You Later
Alee Peoples, 2023
Wool, satin, hand embroidery
70" x 60"

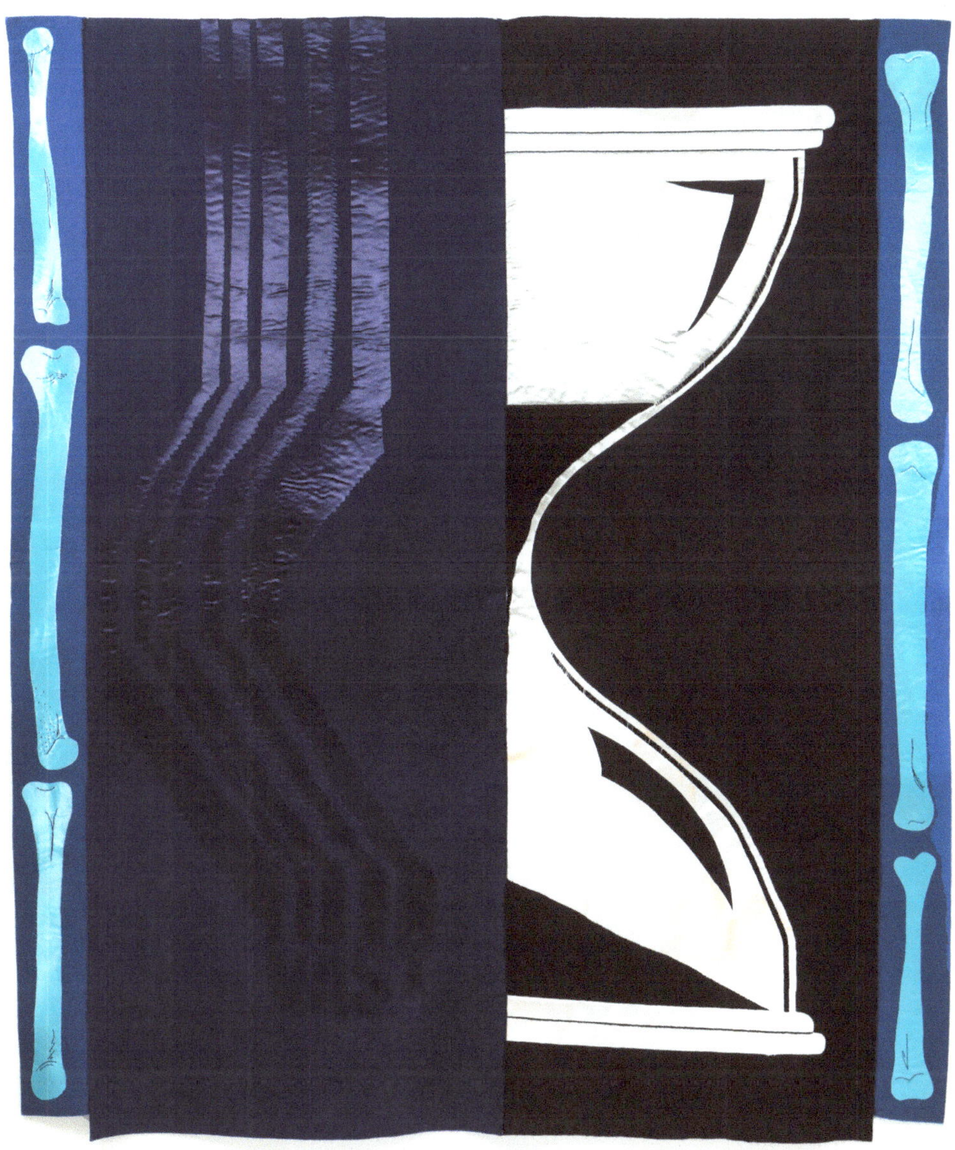

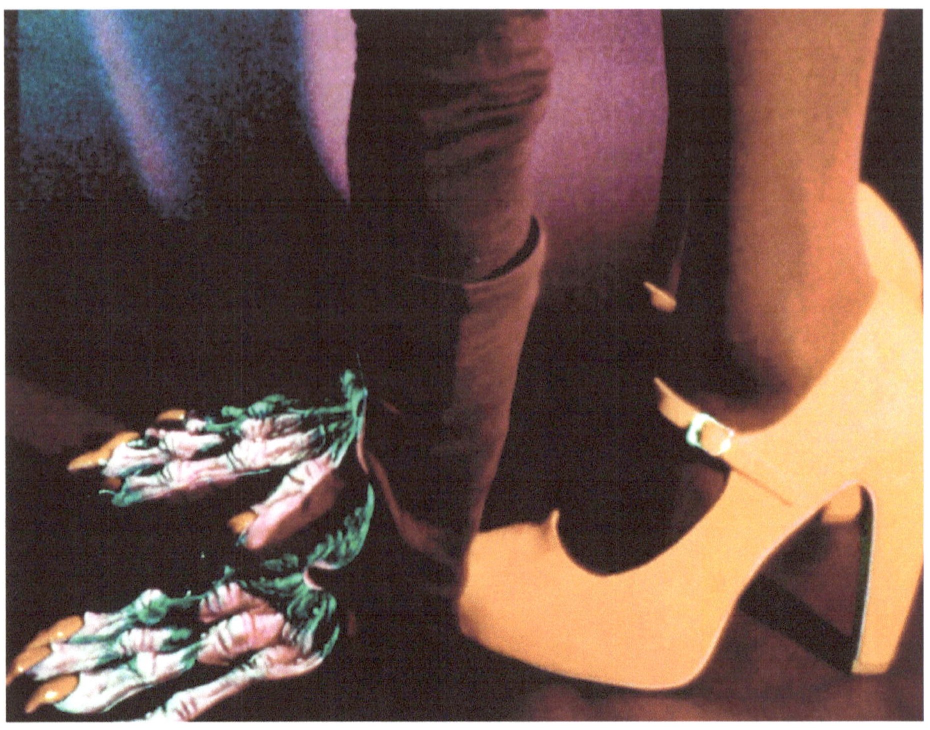

still from ***Standing Forward Full***
Alee Peoples, 2020
16mm film on video
5:38 minutes

stills from ***Non-Stop Beautiful Ladies***
Alee Peoples, 2015
16mm film on video
9:00 minutes

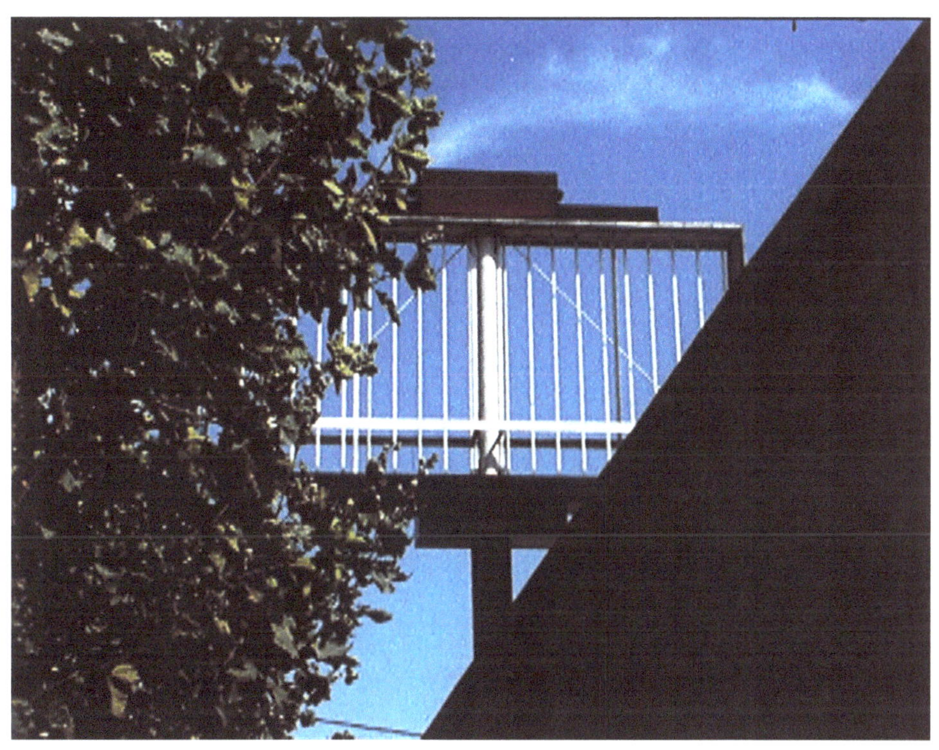

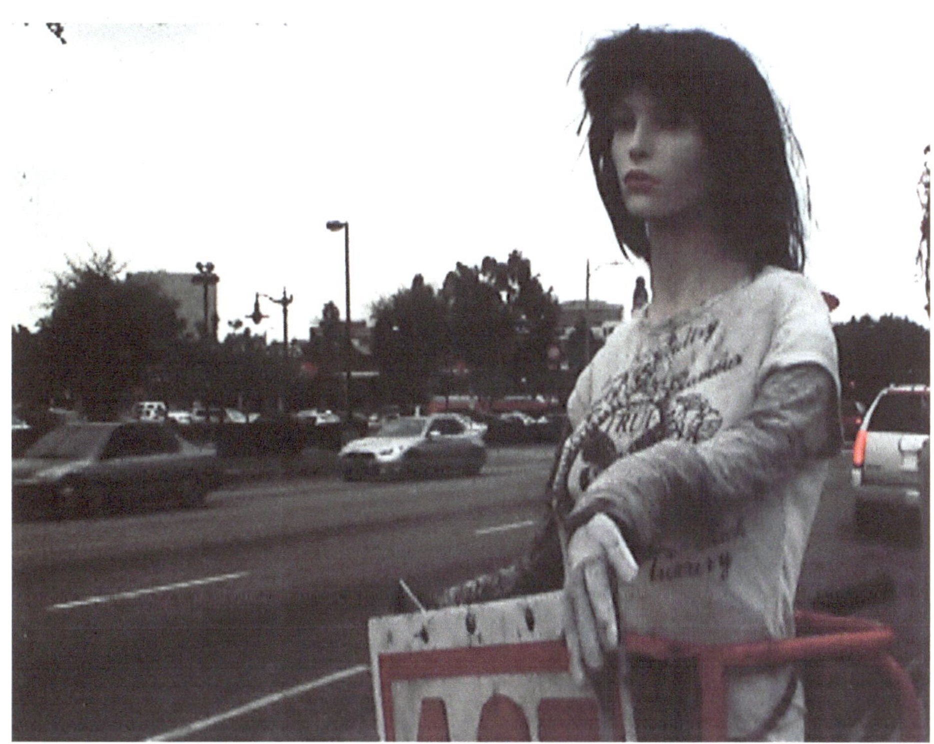

Transcript—Episode 82

The People

Guests—

Alee Peoples
and
Cara Levine

Hosted by Ben White
and
Mathew Timmons

January 18, 2020

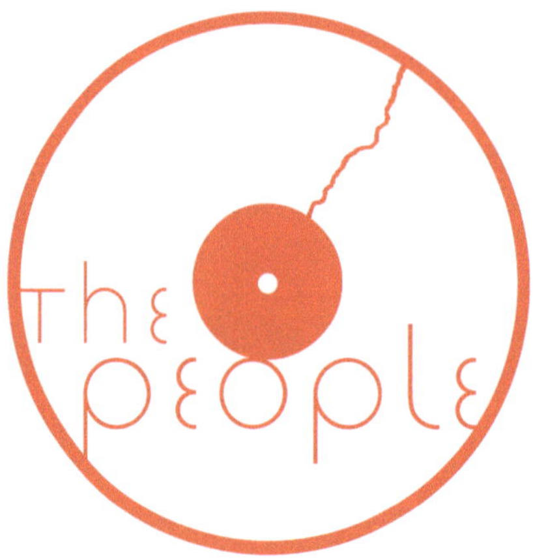

The People, hosted by Mathew Timmons and Ben White was an arts and literature podcast produced by Insert Press in Los Angeles, California. The People produced 84 episodes running from March 2013 to March 2020. All episodes were also broadcast on the 3rd Sunday of each month on KCHUNG 1630 AM. The People featured the voices and ideas of The People that make up the cultural landscape of Los Angeles, the west coast, and beyond … it's like a Broken Record, Magically Repaired.

[Intro Music—Ocfif by Lewis Keller]

M Timmons 0:21
Welcome to Episode 82 of The People on KCHUNG 1630 AM. I'm Mathew Timmons

B White 0:26
and I'm Ben White. Our guests on this episode are Alee Peoples and Cara Levine. Alee Peoples is an artist and filmmaker living in Los Angeles. She's inspired by pedestrian histories, pop song lyrics, and is invested in the handmade. Alee has a film screening on February 22nd at the New Work Salon at Echo Park Film Center right here in LA so you should check that out.

A Peoples 0:50
The props that I make in the film and just camera moves that I do, I'm like, I want it to be very crude and obvious, and I want you to know what those materials are. I want the smoke and mirrors to be really obvious.

M Timmons 1:08
Cara Levine is an artist living in Los Angeles. She works in sculpture, video and socially engaged practices. She has work in the group show Message to Space in the inaugural opening of Supercollider, a new science inspired exhibition platform at the Beacon building here in LA. And also she and Alee have a two person show coming up in April at Elephant Art Space here in the Cypress Park neighborhood of Los Angeles. So you should definitely check that out.

B White 1:32
Yeah, look up Elephant, go there.

C Levine 1:35
I wanted to like undermine my perfectionism as a maker. And I wanted to, really wanted to teach my hands to see, because, also I'm fascinated by like perception and sensitivity and sensorial experience. And it's our hands that, really are our second eyes.

B White 1:54
And at the end of the show, we're gonna go out with a track from friend of the show, Nick Flessa, his new project called Dayton Swim Club.

M Timmons 2:01
The People features the voices and ideas that make up the cultural landscape of Los Angeles, the West Coast and beyond. It's like a broken record, magically repaired.

M Timmons 2:14
Alee Peoples and Cara Levine, welcome to The People.

B White 2:16
Yeah, welcome.

A Peoples 2:17
Thanks so much for having us.

C Levine 2:18
Thanks for having us.

B White 2:19
So, the two of you have a collaborative show at Elephant Art Space in April.

C Levine 2:24
Yes.

B White 2:24
Tell us about that show.

C Levine 2:26
So Alee, and I have a show coming up in April at Elephant Art Space. And it's basically about how each of us in our studios are trying to reconcile impossible truths that we're living with right now, with the 24 hour news cycle, and social media, and I think also just like an over, tidal wave of information and tragedy, be it subtle, ambiguous, or I like, a phrase I like to use is this idea of ambient grief, where we're kind of all swimming together in this knowledge of climate change and

grave change among us. But how do we take this in as artists, slow down and make work to address these things, that is still playful and warm and accessible? But I think that's some of the questions that we're working on in our studios.

A Peoples 3:21
I feel like you more directly deal with them, because your textile pieces are photo based. Pulled from media.

C Levine 3:31
Yeah.

A Peoples 3:32
And you can describe them, your emotional response that you have to them a little better than I can.

C Levine 3:36
Yeah.

A Peoples 3:37
Whereas, but my work? I feel like, while I do have those sentiments and feelings engaging with media, and reconciling that with our ethics, my work, that I think I'm going to show in the, in the Elephant show, is in that world more like escapism, it's more like fantasy based.

C Levine 3:59
Totally...

A Peoples 4:00
Yeah.

C Levine 4:01
It's sort of our different ways of responding to similar issues amongst us. And I think what's exciting about your work is you've developed this whole system of symbols that I think plant escapism and magic and this way that you are using fantasy and illusion to create a different kind of reality. Do you want to talk about that?

A Peoples 4:24
Well, I like that you said symbols because a lot of my work leading up to this was way more like graphic design based and like trying to take apart language and recognizable daily things that we encounter, and like trying to explode them or unpack them or veil them and try and like cognitively, what, how much of a word do we need to, in order to like make that mental leap with it? So I've always worked with language and symbols, but these paintings and drawings are, yes, there's symbols in them, but they're way more like illustrative. And I hadn't painted in like years, by the way, before making this so that these paintings and this new work seems like from the left field or like a U-turn. But they, they of course do relate to my earlier sculpture work and graphic design based work.

M Timmons 4:47
And Alee, you work mainly with film?

A Peoples 5:30
I do all sorts of stuff with sculpture, screen printing, studio based work, not a lot, not a lot of performance...

M Timmons 5:40
Sure.

A Peoples 5:41
And then but yeah, then I do have this whole other practice of 16 millimeter and Super 8 filmmaking, that is on the surface, it seems very removed, but they do relate in that I'm super interested and drawn to material, like handmade material. And so 16 millimeter and Super 8 films I can like, touch the film, and ...

B White 6:04
If you're taking an approach to what Cara was talking about, of like dealing with the situation we all find ourselves in, in America, at least right now. If you're approaching it from an escapist, or using escapist strategies to explore how to get through that, how do you? I guess what I'm wondering is how do you do that without getting too escapist? Or is that even a legit question?

A Peoples 6:28
So I'll just say that, like, these paintings are depictions of something being reflected, which I was doing in my moving image, film work. And you're not sure what the real thing is, like there's a mirroring going on, and the perspective has to be pretty like lined up, because they're very simple in a lot of ways.

B White 6:51
I mean, and Cara, you're not, from looking at your work, it feels like you're also trying to get at an ecstatic truth. Is that, would that be...?

C Levine 7:00
Yeah, I mean, I think that, for both of us, I don't want to speak for you. But I think it's less like, Hey, I'm gonna try to deal with all of these traumas that we're living in right now by burrowing into a hole in my studio and working on these artworks. It's more like this is my actual response. And this is how I am committing my time. And these are the pieces that I'm making. And I think, and inherently we're making them in this context. And so in some ways, it's always responding to that. But one thing that I just wanted to piggyback on is this, the use of language. I think language, for me, it kind of launched the body of work that I'm going to be putting in to our exhibition. And language is a throughline in your work. And even if it's not always there, like in these paintings, you can read them visually, kind of poetically it seems like, they have a kind of inherent secret narrative that you can read into them. So the body of work that I'm putting in is called Fear is a Liar. And it's multi-dimensional, like there's video work, there's textile work, there's drawings, there's all different kinds of pieces of work, but it's all under this umbrella Fear is a Liar. And that language came from me commuting to work one morning, and I was like stuck behind this Penske Truck, that was this big yellow truck. And it was totally painted over in Penske yellow, which was wild, it was like there were no, any other, other markings on it, except for in the very back of the truck, like on the pull down gate, were sticker, stencil letters that said, Fear is a Liar. And I was like, What the fuck is happening? And I trailed behind this truck for like, you know,

20 minutes or something like a chunk of my commute. And I felt like I was in a tunnel with this truck. And I'm a meditator. And there's this idea in meditation where if you use a mantra for 10 days consecutively, like theoretically, you should start to ... change should happen in your body like you should, you should, it should imbue your behavior and your experience. And so I was thinking, while I was watching this truck, it was like during the Kavanaugh hearings, and also the immigration, children are being separated and like the world is ending in a number of different ways. And I'm like, fear is so real. And fear is so truth telling, like fear is so necessary, fear is like a bodily reaction that we live by that is determinant of so much of our behavior, like I don't think fear is a liar. Like I think the idea of fear's a liar is supposed to be this concept of like, you can will yourself to be brave and fear isn't real and fear is tricking you, and it's all made up. And so I'm just like watching this being like, well, will I be more empowered if I don't believe in fear and fear isn't real. I'm just like going through this whole kind of existential crisis with this text, it's so complicated, and it's just on the back of this truck, and like, gosh, like does anybody else see this? I took a bunch of pictures of it, and I took it back to my studio. And one of the first things I did was I wrote the phrase fear is a liar on these big pieces of paper, one a day, repeated for 10 days, in that action of like, trying to repeat it for 10 days. And then I also went back to the first image and then sewed a kind of large scale, like four by five foot textile, where I'm like picking and choosing the parts of this image that were so important to me, and ... kind of reordering it and portraying it as like a hand-sewn object. So it's like kind of slowing down and trying to meditate in a way on this concept more and more, and then it's kind of bled into further, other language explorations and other site specific kind of works. But ...

M Timmons 11:14
So at that point, after 10 days is, is fear a liar?

C Levine 11:19
Yeah, I need more.

A Peoples 11:21
Well and what you were saying about like, I forget what but just the fear is a liar, but, but don't 'cuz you can't let fear at this point in ... you can't be cynical, you can't be apathetic, like ...

C Levine 11:36
Right.

A Peoples 11:36
So if you're afraid of shit, in this time, like ...

C Levine 11:40
Yeah, it feels like a really complicated phrase. It's like, No, you can't be, but did you say, you can't be empathetic?

A Peoples 11:48
You can't be apathetic. Yeah, thank you.

C Levine 11:52
Yeah, yeah. Right. You can't be apathetic. But like our fear reaction is being triggered so often, right, like, in so many ways, like just driving alone, you know, like you're in, you have to be so alert, and like, and then on the news and in relationships, and like fear is so ever present?

A Peoples 12:11
Well, I know you've done a few projects where you like, write people or call people or introduce yourself to people, right. And I, as a very shy person, I'm like, I need to pay attention to that.

B White 12:21
Oh yeah, you wrote Adrian Piper.

C Levine 12:22
I wrote Adrian Piper, I actually sent Adrian Piper, a 45 minute video of myself, speaking to one of her pieces, asking her to sit with me, but she never wrote me back. But in graduate school, I will say, to my credit was not, that was not a cold call. There have been many cold calls, but she and I had a correspondence for about a year. And it was really impactful

for me. She's one of my art heroes, and I wrote her as a student, like, from the perspective of like, you are my art hero, and I'm seeking counsel from you. And she was so gracious and, and gave me great counsel during that time, but she never responded to my video.

A Peoples 13:08
But the piece you responded to was repetitive and meditative.

C Levine 13:12
Yeah, yeah. But yeah, and I also once wrote 35 letters to an artist who just turned 100 named Pierre Soulages who's a painter. Because I was interested in darkness, I was exploring darkness in my work a lot. And he spent seven years painting abstract expressionist paintings in black. And also, he never wrote back. But ...

A Peoples 13:36
This guy knows about darkness.

C Levine 13:38
He knows, I was like, you know a lot about darkness. So yeah, there's a, there's definitely like an interest in my work in following a problem and trying to address it at different angles until I understand it better. Like, the labor that I put into the work is a part of the work itself, which I think is true for a lot of artists, right. And actually, I think it's probably indicative of your filmmaking method, you know, like your, the way that you, the way that you structure and shoot and then edit your film seems really process dependent and both intentional, highly intentional, and also has room for spontaneity.

A Peoples 14:22
Yeah. I don't want that to be on the surface, though. You know?

C Levine 14:28
What do you mean?

A Peoples 14:29
Well, I was thinking about, because a lot of your performance

based work or even your carvings, the, I think the, the process and the journey of it is the destination, right? for you.

C Levine 14:42
That's right, but your work, It's like, here's the piece, and the process is like a part of it, but it's not forefronted.

A Peoples 14:50
Yeah, yeah. I don't know. I think anything that you make by hand takes time.

B White 14:55
Isn't there an element of not arriving in some of your work that I've seen, someone landing, or almost landing, but never landing. Tell me the piece that I'm thinking of ...

A Peoples 15:03
Oh yeah, yeah that's an older piece. I don't know that was just me fucking with like rhythm and repetition and well that, that's a great like film technique or something where you just, you cut ...

B White 15:19
before the thing happens

A Peoples 15:20
... in the middle, before they hit the ground and they're like suspended in air if you repeat it over like 10 times yeah,

B White 15:27
Yeah well when Cara said not, like the phrase not arriving that reminded me of

A Peoples 15:31
Got it yeah, literally not arriving on the ground.

B White 15:34
The specific import of the moment like never actually happening.

C Levine 15:40
But that is also happening in these paintings in some way too like, there's a mystery in each of them there's no figures in them, and there's, in these paintings of yours, there's no, you know, there's like the, it, what appears to have been like a trace of a person, like with the candles, for example, like those candles were lit by somebody, but there's no somebody there and those candles are sort of floating.

A Peoples 16:06
Yeah.

C Levine 16:07
So there is kind of, I haven't really ever thought about it that way, but that kind of not arriving. It seems sort of relevant.

A Peoples 16:14
Yeah, there's a bunch of motion going on too like, there's objects that are like about to touch each other or are flying through the air, and so like direction is implied. And the titles are pretty, for someone who's always hated titling artworks, these paintings have like really long sentence narrative titles that imply a ton of narrative to them.

C Levine 16:43
I love titles like that.

A Peoples 16:44
Good.

[Interstitial Music—Ocfif by Lewis Keller]

B White 16:48
You are listening to The People on KCHUNG 1630 AM. I'm Ben White.

M Timmons 16:53
And I'm Mathew Timmons. You can find The People every third Sunday at 3pm on KCHUNG 1630 AM and or wherever you find your podcasts, everywhere, all the places ...

B White 17:05
Yeah, go to Apple podcasts or Stitcher or SoundCloud or any of that stuff...

M Timmons 17:09
All those things...

B White 17:10
Search for the people radio and find us there.

M Timmons 17:12
And you can also find us on Instagram at the_people_radio, and you can find information about all of our episodes there. And you can find us on SoundCloud.

B White 17:23
Oh, you can also find us on InsertBlancPress.net

M Timmons 17:26
Oh, yeah.

B White 17:26
... by clicking on The People at the top of the page. And that's got all the episodes.

M Timmons 17:31
You can find us everywhere.

B White 17:32
Yeah. So come around, see us sometime.

M Timmons 17:34
Exactly. And now back to our conversation with Alee Peoples and Cara Levine.

C Levine 17:40
Alee, I wanted to ask you about your recent time you spent in Alaska.

A Peoples 17:45
So I just did a residency called Chulitna Lodge, and it is on

Lake Clark in Southcentral Alaska. And by bush plane it's an hour west of Anchorage.

B White 17:45
Oh, yeah. bush plane. Sure.

A Peoples 18:01
Yeah, bush plane. So Alaska is massive and huge and there aren't roads anywhere, and a lot of people own planes, or know pilots or are a pilot of small single engine or double engine planes are very common there, and that's just how people get around. And there's a very small residency there on Lake Clark, and they have funding and they operate between, I'm gonna say May through mid October. But I was there for six weeks, and it was really crazy to go somewhere so remote, like I really felt like I was looking down the barrel, and like I'm checked out, like I dove in. And it was really great, but also really difficult.

B White 18:56
Well, how do they, how do they set you up with like a place to live, obviously.

A Peoples 18:59
Yeah, so everyone gets a cabin that can also double as your studio but you are free to carve out other studio space. They're nice cabins, but spartan in some ways. And then there's a large lodge where they provide meals so there's a chef or two there cooking meals for you. And at any given time there's four to six artists in residence along with I'll say six staff members that are just taking care of the property, the buildings, laundry, making sure you have the tools you need, taking care of the generator and the solar panels...

C Levine 19:45
Is it off the grid then?

A Peoples 19:47
It's off the grid, it is generator run so they're toggling back and forth between diesel run generator and that then feeds a battery and then solar. But when I was there it was overcast

at least half the time so the solar was, was not kicking in, but that is running and they do have like a hydro power thing that they're going to install in the creek.

B White 20:16
Well, how do you, how do you make work there? And what kind of work did you make?

A Peoples 20:23
Very portable, I took watercolors and I took a borrowed laptop to work on a soundtrack.

C Levine 20:31
Right.

A Peoples 20:31
Yeah, I didn't want to haul things I didn't want to ship things

C Levine 20:34
You had to bring all your own materials and all your own tools.

A Peoples 20:36
Yeah, I took a book, like they have a library, but I took the milepost book to help me get around afterwards.

C Levine 20:45
And it was isolating.

A Peoples 20:47
It was super isolating. So they, but they do have internet, but it is like, slow, and I'll just honestly, like, there were times where I was like, I would rather not even have the idea of the internet. No phone service. So yeah, it was just really difficult to be like that isolated, but surrounded by really intense untouched beauty and nature.

M Timmons 21:19
And May to October was not terribly cold, or?

A Peoples 21:23
It was not terribly cold. So very sunny. I feel like I timed it,

like just right because I love fall. Salmon season is, I'm a little confused by this, but the salmon run I think happened in July. So the salmon are like spawning right out the front door, which is amazing. So then they just have this stock supply of salmon for you to enjoy and eat. But yeah, as soon as I showed up, the leaves were turning. And then at the tail end, there was snow on the mountains.

B White 21:55
I think that's what everyone who lives in a big metropolitan area imagines that they want to do at all moments, right? Especially like to go to one of those places and be provided with a space to make work, right. Is that the case? Or was it so isolating that it was hard to operate?

A Peoples 22:13
No, it was super luxurious. And that like, it's kind of disgusting, like you wake up, you go have breakfast and like, it's unstructured time. So I would read and then go into the cabin and like paint or think for six hours. Within that time, I would walk to the river, that's a 20 minute walk, or walk to the marsh, that's a 20 minute... Like, you can go zone out in nature, and then come back. I did really stick to a structure just to help me so then I would like stretch before dinner, like I knew that they blow a conch shell for dinner at seven. So I knew that was coming. And then you have dinner with everyone, like a communal dinner. And then part of the deal is you're on dish duty. There's a lot of fucking dishes. So many dishes.

C Levine 23:06
Good thing they have four to six residents.

A Peoples 23:08
A lot of dishes, like but I got into it, and then yeah, I don't know. But only being able to like walk 20 minutes in either direction before you encounter a body of water or like debilitating mountain was tough. And my dad was like, hope you're finding your way around like sending you some money to spend on like...

C Levine 23:31
There's no around and around.

A Peoples 23:32
There's no, yeah, I got it. Yeah, I got it.

C Levine 23:35
Yeah, it's an interesting conceit, I think, this idea that as artists living in a city, this kind of fantasy to go to a rural or secluded, isolated place and think that suddenly in a way that will free us up creatively with sort of this romantic vision, and in some ways it possibly could and inspire a lot of new thoughts and different thoughts and make space for different kind of growth as an artist and also just give you plain old time, like time that you did not have...

A Peoples 24:07
It's so nice

C Levine 24:07
in your regular hustle.

A Peoples 24:09
I will say...

B White 24:10
That's the main sell right?

C Levine 24:10
That's the main sell.

A Peoples 24:11
Yeah,

M Timmons 24:12
Extra time

A Peoples 24:12
Having your meals made for you...

C Levine 24:15
It's a huge difference.

A Peoples 24:16
...is a huge help like I spend so much time you know, buying and making meals. Just having that taken care of was, was amazing.

B White 24:24
Tell us, the both of you, because I know you're both residency type artists. How do you reconcile that with the buying of food when you're home like and making a living and surviving financially? How do you figure that out?

A Peoples 24:39
I'm a super freak and like make a lot of meals and I don't know what, like I do enjoy eating out, but I just want to be in control of what I eat and feel good.

C Levine 24:50
Me too, I cook basically all my meals and I'll buy for the week and prepare and then for me it's like the measure that I'm, that's hardest for me to gain control of is my time, the unobstructed time in the studio. Like, in city life, in daily life when I'm working and teaching and have my dog and have laundry and food and expenses and all the things like the studio time, no matter how much you space it out, doesn't feel expansive in the same way as unobstructed residency time. It's such a gift. And I also like to make it really structured when I do have an opportunity to be on residency because it's like, this is such an indulgence. And it's like, I'm so lucky to have this time, I'm just going to use the shit out of it for work. But it's, I think to answer your question, it's just such a balance that we're all trying to figure out how do we manage our time and our expenses and putting our body in the specific place that it needs to be in, in that time, in LA?

A Peoples 25:58
Yeah.

B White 25:59
Right. Because it's not just having the unstructured studio time. It's not being so exhausted, that you want to lay down and die when that unstructured time arrives.

C Levine 26:07
Yeah, and that you should, it's like, great, like, we deserve to go to work, and come home and like brain drain. It's a crazy expectation that we have of each other, of ourselves, to go home, go to work and then go to work again. Right.

B White 26:22
It's a second job.

C Levine 26:24
Yeah.

B White 26:24
For sure.

A Peoples 26:24
Yeah.

C Levine 26:26
It's the first job, and then all of our jobs for money are our second job, Yeah, you know, yeah. I think.

A Peoples 26:33
And cooking for me at home is such a reset, like, way more than exercise. Yeah, like, I have to go home and cook. Because if I don't, I'll feel like I'm out of control. I don't know what it is. But if I like buy two lunches out in a row, I feel very chaotic. And I do not like that. It's not that I can't afford it...

C Levine 26:55
Yeah, I also learned something when I was really young, when I was 18. I worked for an artist for a year, and we always took breaks for lunch. And she was the first artist I ever worked for. And she was Spanish. And we always had a significant like lunch break, that was some time. And multiple things happened on the lunch break, like you would have lunch,

maybe you would tidy up, maybe you would take a little nap or, but it was like a distinct period of time that was like a grace period between the morning work and the afternoon work.

B White 27:32
It is incredible to think about the idea of art making as primarily a time management strategy. Like if it's going to be possible to be an artist like that entails a very strict regimen of time management. Yeah, right. And financial management. And those are the same often right? Right.

A Peoples 27:51
You just have to be on it, though, because I like will go to studio and just space out.

B White 27:58
Sure.

A Peoples 27:59
Or I'll go to studio just to eat sometimes.

B White 28:01
But that feels like a victory.

C Levine 28:02
Or you'll go to studio just to answer emails, right?

B White 28:05
But you're in there, and that's like, but I did it.

A Peoples 28:08
Yeah.

B White 28:08
I've won. I did the thing.

A Peoples 28:09
I got my body in the studio, but my mind is still outside.

C Levine 28:13
Or sometimes what happens to me now is like, some of the

work that I'm working on, the physical actual artwork is very slow. And I'll be like, god dammit, this is so slow, I could be sending off a bajillion emails right now, or whatever. And it takes me a while to like drop back into, then that's the sort of rhythm, time thing it's like, if I'm hustling and at my jobs and teaching and all these things, then I get to the studio and I have two hours to carve, those hours, first of all, it's really hard for my brain to be like now you're in carving time, which is really slow, and then, so there's that and then also I know not that much happens in two hours. So I, yeah, it's just this, this calculation and calibration all the time.

B White 29:02
Do you feel like you were prepared for that at school? Anyone prepared you for that sort of thing? of just being like, you need to get into the studio, every single hour and just be working until you fall asleep?

A Peoples 29:14
Yeah, there was that? For sure. Or like if you were seen outside of studio relaxing, people would be like, What are you, what's wrong with you? You're ready, be like, yeah, I'm ready...

C Levine 29:25
Right. Right. Like if you aren't like strung out...

A Peoples 29:28
...bleeding out of your eyes, you aren't a good artist. And I was like, I'm not subscribing to that.

C Levine 29:34
Yeah, I would get really, this is, I don't know how it's gonna go over, but I would get really health, hyper aware in grad school right before the end, like major critiques or my graduate exhibition. And I would like get on a super strict diet, and I would make sure I exercised and make sure I slept. And everyone else is like, dying out there. They're like, strung out, they're drunk. They're like never sleeping. They're like splayed all over the studio floor. And I'd be like, I'm gonna, I'm on a nine to five thing here because also in school it's such a gift like you, that's, that's basically what you're doing. I had a part

time job, but I could be nine to five at studio. But to answer your question, the same artist that I worked for when I was a teenager, I, I moved out of the country when I was a teenager to work, to try to... Well, I moved to Spain, like a kind of crazy person with some money I saved, and I had found an artist to work for, and I had a very traditional master-apprentice relationship for a year, which I forget how it influenced me and continues to influence me. But even before college, I was, I learned so much from her about how to be a practicing artist, and about showing up at the studio every day, and making food and bringing food and feeding the cat, turning the heater on, which was a fire, and, and that, Marisa like really taught me a lot of discipline about just the daily labor of what it takes to do that. So when I started college, I was kind of much more prepared in some ways for what it meant to make art, I think, than college students. That sustained me a lot.

A Peoples 31:30
I remember about being in grad school, and in some ways I don't think this is the best way to make art as you get older and develop your processes, but like, in school, you have to crank stuff out...

C Levine 31:44
Totally.

A Peoples 31:44
...and making 16 millimeter films in school. I was on it. I was like, I gotta go buy an axe. I gotta call this person and make sure they're ready by two on Thursday. Like I could just like, yeah, hammer it out, and crank them out. And I try to remind myself that...

C Levine 32:03
It's so much harder now.

A Peoples 32:05
It is, but I don't know. Yeah, it's a constant like, you got to find the balance.

[Interstitial Music—Ocfif by Lewis Keller]

M Timmons 32:13
You're listening to The People on KCHUNG 1630 AM. I'm Mathew Timmons.

B White 32:17
And I'm Ben White. Remember, you can listen to us every third Sunday at 3pm on KCHUNG 1630 AM, or of course find us anywhere where you get your pods.

M Timmons 32:26
Everywhere that you get your podcasts, you will find us there. And if you listen to the show and you like it, tell a friend, leave a rating or a review

B White 32:35
Yeah, and all that helps us out, or find us on Instagram at the_people_radio.

M Timmons 32:41
Find us there.

B White 32:43
And now we'll get back to our conversation with Alee Peoples and Cara Levine

A Peoples 32:48
Cara when you were in Spain, is that where you learned?... you were doing carving with this artist or...

C Levine 32:56
So, when I was in Spain, I was working for an artist, a Spanish artist who herself had a teacher who passed on to her these like hundreds years old Spanish Arabic luster glazes and when I went I had, I was going under the premises that I wanted to learn pottery or ceramics more deeply. So I was making these glazes for her and firing her kilns, but she also worked in plastic so we did a lot of like pouring resin. And then also she taught me a little bit of stone carving and gave me my first carving gloves and my first couple chisels. So yeah, I did learn a little bit about how to hold tools and use them.

A Peoples 33:40
Because you have this whole side of your practice that is carving but I know to be in wood.

C Levine 33:46
Yeah, wood is a lot easier to carve than stone.

M Timmons 33:48
Yeah.

C Levine 33:50
I would like to actually at some point get back into or learn more like, formidably learn how to carve stone but yeah, I slowly as like kind of a throughline for the last 15 years in my practice, I've been carving and wood continues to be a material that I find I have access to and is really a joy to work with. And I think I learned to carve wood on this epic trip that I used to take with my ex and another couple where we would go to this island in the Bahamas and, that had been farmed for lumber and had all this old growth mahogany and pine. And we would go into the, into these old growth forests where they had, many of the trees had fallen, and would take a chainsaw and we would just cut out mahogany and bring it to the beach and bring to these sawhorses we had kind of set up and just carve all day every day. Like bowls and weird objects and wood cuts for prints, and fish and eat and camp and I really learned kind of how to, like what a good ribbon feels like when you're carving, like, what does it feel like when your tools are sharp? How do you sharpen your tools? How do you hold your tools? How do you stand? And all of those kinds of like methods, just like to understand the craft of it without having to, without the pressure of making something unique or an art object.

A Peoples 35:19
As a non-carver I totally understood what you meant when you said a good ribbon.

C Levine 35:25
Okay, yeah, right. Yeah, totally.

A Peoples 35:26
Yeah, so satisfying.

C Levine 35:28
It's so satisfying. And are you pushing the chisel? Are you using a mallet on the chisel? Like, how are you making your cuts? And what's the angle of the cut? And

A Peoples 35:37
but then, when you were living in Oakland, you, and correct me if I'm wrong, but you started to work with artists with disabilities?

C Levine 35:45
Yeah, definitely. I, when I was in graduate school, I had my first, I had an internship, a work study kind of program at a studio called NIAD in Richmond. And there, I worked with artists with developmental disabilities. And I was the ceramics teacher, because clay was always my first material, and my most kind of familial material, familiar material. And so I was a, well actually at NIAD I wasn't, I was a mixed media teacher, but then after grad school, I worked at Creative Growth Art Center for three years in Oakland. And I was the ceramics teacher. And they actually really taught me to unlearn basically, everything I thought I knew about clay, which was really an expansive experience. Like you can fire anything, all these potters out there, like it has to be hollow, and you know, just, it doesn't have to be hollow. You just have to take your time and, and heat the kiln very, very, very, very slowly and carefully.

A Peoples 36:52
But I remember you doing, and I haven't seen this in person, but you did like a blind contour carving of a pillow.

C Levine 36:58
Yes, yes. So yeah, that was inspired by working with these artists. That's a good memory. So I was working at Creative Growth. And I had this really great artist that I worked with named David Parsons, who continues to be one of my favorite artists. And he is basically blind. He can see a little

bit if he brings something very close to his eyes, but it's sort of constantly moving, constantly moving vision. And I was really inspired by his method because he was really craft oriented, detail oriented, and would try to make these kind of hyper realistic animal drawings and also clay objects that were animals like dogs and birds. And what would happen is, it looked like the bird or the animal was kind of moving, because he would look at the picture and then go back to the sculpture that he was working on, and look at the picture and go back to the sculpture. And the sculpture would kind of evolve as his vision with it would. And it was really a touch oriented object. And I was like, I want my hands to see the way that his hands see. And so I went on a residency in Colorado, and we had this amazing sculpture facility, and I decided I was going to carve two objects. They were pillows out of wood and I hadn't ever, I hadn't carved a wooden sculpture yet. Ever. Take that back. There was one in grad school. But anyway, so I was gonna carve two objects, and they're gonna be pillows. And I decided to make two blanks that were the same blanks, just like on the bandsaw roughing them out. And then I carved one with sight, copying a pillow in the studio, you know, however laborious that was. And then I blindfolded myself, I actually sandblasted my safety glasses.

A Peoples 38:56
Oh, you're so smart.

C Levine 38:57
You know, protect your eyes while you're blinding yourself. And I, so I sandblasted my safety glasses. And then I also, while I did it, I was so distracted. aurally like by sound...

A Peoples 39:12
For sure.

C Levine 39:12
...that I also had to cover my ears. So and then I used the other, the first carved pillow as my guide and I would touch it with my hands. And then I would move over to my new pillow. And I would try to replicate those, those lines, those sort of veins and ripples in the fabric, blinded and I was just

curious, like, I wanted to undermine my perfectionism as a maker. And, and I wanted to, really wanted to teach my hands to see because also I'm fascinating, fascinated by like perception and sensitivity and sensorial experience and it's our hands like that really are our second eyes like babies and kids, they depend on their hands to see so much, to orient yourself in space to catch yourself if you fall. And we're like, more and more out of touch with, with touch, but it's another conversation. But for me like, yeah, I, I wanted to replicate these, this thing blindfolded. And then it was such a challenge. I have this kind of personal rule that if I do something challenging once, it's kind of a fluke, so I have to do it twice. So I made a second set, later at home in my studio that were of floaties like swimming floaties

A Peoples 40:37
You couldn't live with the first set?

C Levine 40:41
That was like, I didn't want...

A Peoples 40:42
A practice...

B White 40:43
It's not proof. It's, you know?

C Levine 40:45
Yeah. I figured, yeah, I don't know. I have. Don't you have weird rules that you live by like...?

A Peoples 40:50
Sure.

B White 40:51
I guess this is a good question for you, Alee, because you use, I mean, you do film, you do sculpture, you do fabric stuff, you do sewing stuff, you do everything. So what is, what is your relationship to these to, to the form of a piece like to materials, how do you choose and why do you? Why do you choose the thing that you choose?

A Peoples 41:10
Oh, oftentimes, I'm like putting the cart before the horse. It's super material based. It's a little, it's actually way different with the film. I don't know there's, there's all sorts of like references going on there like I'll get excited about a reference and then just move forward with the material. I feel like that's changing and like getting way more expansive. Now that I don't know the, the paintings are putting me in this whole different like mind space, which is good. I think..

C Levine 41:42
She's like, I learned I'm a killer painter.

A Peoples 41:44
That's loaded, it's actually like kind of embarrassing. Like I have painter friends and I'm like, I can paint, I'm painting. Anyone can fucking paint. It's fine. Yeah, I don't know. And then the films, they're very material based not only in getting to hold the actual film and the cameras as an apparatus, and like an extension of the body, which I think you could pick up on. But the props that I make in the film and just camera moves that I do, I'm like, I want it to be very crude and obvious. And I want you to know what those materials are. I want the smoke and mirrors to be really obvious.

C Levine 42:32
Yeah, it's like a broken fourth wall.

A Peoples 42:34
Exactly.

C Levine 42:35
Yeah, yeah.

B White 42:36
Well, so we should talk about, Cara, your project, This is Not a Gun. Tell us about that project.

C Levine 42:43
Thank you. Um, yeah. So for the last three years, I've basically been immersed in a project in my studio that has jumped

out of my studio into the community called This is Not a Gun. And it started with my carving, kind of carving practice. And it started in the winter of 2016, after Trump was elected. And we were all in this kind of walking around like zombies phase. But simultaneously, one thing that was happening more and more in the news is many, many unarmed innocent black men were being murdered by police. And I had been living in Oakland, and had recently moved to Portland, Oregon at this time, but my community at home was really in an uproar, and I felt really powerless. And this was sort of on my mind, but I saw a Harper's Magazine, Harper's Magazine, Instagram feed piece or something that...

A Peoples 43:46
Like a list, it makes full lists.

C Levine 43:49
Exactly. It was a list a Harper's list. And it was called, Trigger Warning, These objects have all been mistaken as guns by police officers in shootings of unarmed civilians. It had a list of 23 objects. They're very ubiquitous, set of keys, cell phone, wallet, sandwich, Bible, and hand, cane. And I actually felt really angry at this not just, of course, the first shock of like, Oh, my God, all these objects, but really, like there was an error in the publishing, it felt like really thoughtless in some ways, it was missing all the relevant information. Who are these people? What are their names? Where do they come from? What is their race? You know, and we can kind of intuit because we're culturally sensitive people, but we don't know, this information is not here. And it felt like clickbait and it felt like shock. This like shock oriented propaganda or something. So I wanted to spend more time with these objects and understand more thoroughly what was happening. So I'm trying to tell the story quickly because it's a long story, but so I started in my studio, carving the objects that had been on the list out of wood. And in that process, I also had been going through a process of re-learning re-educating myself about the history of race in the United States, through text and rhetoric, listening while I carved. And then very quickly, it was like, this is, this, this work, this is my devotional labor, kind of, for somebody else's loss. But it's not my loss, it's not my story. And I really wanted it to

have a greater, be a part of a greater conversation. And so I started hosting these ceramic based workshops in different community centers and art spaces. And I co-host with different women, all women of color, who are invested in race equity work, through their work, whether it's art or activism or healing work. And we make the work in clay. And then we hold a conversation about these things, race equity, cultural trauma...

A Peoples 45:53
With, excuse me, participants that come just through word of mouth and like promotion...

C Levine 45:58
...totally, public, and often in the last few, really aiming towards working with teenagers. That's my favorite audience to work with. And often the teenagers will help lead the workshops in the conversation because they're having a different conversation than we are. Yeah, so this has kind of like grown into a project all on its own that has, I now have dozens of collaborators and I've worked in lots of different cities. And I've created a zine with an artist in Oakland named Lukaza Branfman-Verissimo, to try to extend this workshop template for other communities to host. And I will plug also in 2020, I'm super stoked, we have a book coming out about the project that has 38 different contributors, each contributor is writing about their own experience with one of these objects. So for me, the multitude of these stories kind of undermines the idea that any of these objects could be seen as a threat. And of course, also, I've done all the research on all of the victims that are on this list, and know their names, and their stories, and all of that is shared information, something we talk about at the workshops. It's hard to talk about this project quickly, in some ways, because it has to unpack in a group conversation. It takes time. And there's a lot of muddy conversation around race and whiteness, and trauma that comes up. And it's worth spending the time with, it's really, it needs a lot of time.

B White 47:36
And people should check that out online.

C Levine 47:38
Yeah, there's a website. Thisisnotagun.com. It has its own website.

B White 47:41
Everyone go there. And while we're talking about community engagement, Alee really quick in our time...

A Peoples 47:46
Yeah...

B White 47:47
...plug that Echo Park Film Center and tell us about your involvement.

A Peoples 47:50
Well, Echo Park Film Center is an amazing place that is going on 18, 19 years, I should know because they just had their anniversary. But there are very many things there, a classroom for little to no cost for young people and older people. They rent equipment, super 8, 16, video, they rent DVDs, they rent, film prints, maybe books. They have a small school bus that goes around to communities that are far away from Echo Park that would take someone like a long time to get to, to use the resources there. And they're also a micro-cinema, I'll say three nights a week, maybe even more. They have community based video, film screenings, they're open to collaborating, you can rent the place. It's really insane the amount of stuff that they've done, that they've done, and just the people that get involved with it. And they're really invested in like putting the tools of the moving image in other people's hands. I couldn't say enough great things.

B White 49:02
Yeah, everyone should go online and check them out. That's, of course in the Echo Park neighborhood here in Los Angeles.

A Peoples 49:07
Yes.

B White 49:08
Both you and, we're not going to go this whole podcast

without saying Mike Stoltz name, say it...

A Peoples 49:13
Mike Stoltz!... Very many, well so many people help out with that place. They've since moved to a co-op model. So there's about 20 artists that helped run that space now. Yeah, they're on Alvarado, just I'll say north of Sunset. And well, so one micro-cinema thing that happens is Dicky Bahto, who's an amazing force there has been doing a screening series called The New Work Salons. And they started by just him casually wanting to see his friends work, because we're all making work all the time, but it's not often curated into a screening around town. So he, as he, he keeps in touch with everyone and just knows that when we've finished a piece that we're welcome to show it in these screenings called New Work Salons. They're not curated, which is like refreshing, and there's no Q&A, which was also refreshing. You are encouraged to talk about it. Yeah. But yeah, you're not held prisoner at the end of the screening. So yeah, it's always great, I'm always thankful to show my new work there, but it, so I just finished a new film. That's five and a half minutes long and that will show in the February New Work Salon on the 22nd.

B White 49:24
Yeah.

C Levine 49:24
Are my ankles in it?

A Peoples 50:31
Ooh, your ankles and your hands.

C Levine 50:33
Really?

A Peoples 50:33
Yes.

C Levine 50:34
Made the cut!

B White 50:35
You finally made it.

C Levine 50:37
I've never been in one.

B White 50:38
You finally made it.

A Peoples 50:39
Oh, you're in.

B White 50:40
Well, Alee, Cara, Thank you so much for joining us.

M Timmons 50:42
Thank you.

A Peoples 50:43
Thanks for having us.

M Timmons 50:44
Thank you.

[Interstitial Music—Ocfif by Lewis Keller]

B White 50:46
You've been listening to Episode 82 of The People on KCHUNG 1630 AM. I'm Ben White.

M Timmons 50:51
And I'm Mathew Timmons. You can find all of our past episodes, that's 81 plus this one, 82 episodes, all of our past episodes at InsertBlancPress.net by clicking The People at the top of the page.

B White 51:04
or anywhere else you get your podcasts

M Timmons 51:05
everywhere

B White 51:06
we're there, search for The People Radio, you know go to the Instagram the_people_radio.

M Timmons 51:12
All the people, all the places.

B White 51:13
Our interstitial music is as always Ocfif by Louis Keller.

M Timmons 51:17
Yep. Louis, thank you again so much for that.

B White 51:20
And we're gonna go out with the latest from friend of the show, Nick Flessa. It's a single that came out last month under the name, Dayton Swim Club and that's inspired by a cult, early internet video of the same name. Project stems from Nick Flessa Band, but it's more collaborative this round and it features Mario Luna on guitar. I hope I get everyone's name right. Jessica Perelman, Jessica I hope that's right, on drums, and Kirsten Bladh of the band Leggy, on bass and Dominique Matelson, Dominique I apologize if I fucked that up, on backing vocals and keys and the name of the song is Rage All Night

[Music—Rage All Night by Dayton Swim Club]

www.ingramcontent.com/pod-product-compliance
Lightning Source LLC
LaVergne TN
LVHW070226110826
845147LV00003B/655

* 9 7 8 1 9 4 7 3 2 2 0 6 6 *